The Pandemic Notes Workbook was launched online in February 2021.
500 copies were printed in June 2021. You can find it online at
https://pandemic-notes.maydayrooms.org/workbook/

ISBN: 978-1-838485 1 - 1 -5

Distributed for free by **PM Press UK**.

This workbook has been produced as an educational resource. If you have any issues with the
contents email us at in-formation@maydayrooms.org

Contents

'Why did it take the UK government eight weeks
to recognise the seriousness of what we now call Covid19?'
The editor of The Lancet asks.
129 fake NHS workers' Twitter accounts back Boris:
Reality management over real management.
They manufacture consent but there's no PPE.

'Facing the danger of market segregation,
at that moment humanity needs some government to make a case for freedom of exchange,
some country to take off its Clark Kent spectacles
and to emerge as the supercharged champion of the rights of populations of the earth
to buy and sell freely among each other,'
said Johnson in February.
Panic buying toilet paper,
there was lot of shit to wipe;
entrepreneurs bought gallons of hand sanitiser and sold them on eBay at a tidy profit.
The roads that Spring were quiet and, for once, we heard the birds.

OPEC & Russia cut oil production by a tenth and still the price remained negative.
At an IMF meeting, it was announced that 10 countries (in Asia and Africa)
spent more than 20% of government revenue on external debt payments in 2019.
'This is a message from Neath Port Talbot council' said a drone,
'please follow the government rules at this time. You must stay at home.'

Boris rose from the dead on Easter Sunday
at a time of reverse triage when the morgues had overflown and body bags run out.
Our elders were taken from us.
Call centres, and the hidden factories of capitalism got outbreaks of virus.
In the US, McDonalds and Amazon workers went on strike.

People denounced their wives and neighbours for breaking lockdown
and some prisoners were released.

An anarchist was interviewed about mutual aid groups on a TV breakfast show.
The presenters asked with amazement,
'what were you doing before this to have the initiative to do that?
What gave you that idea?'

'Behind the disciplinary mechanisms can be read the haunting memory of "contagions",
of the plague, of rebellions, crimes, vagabondage, desertions,
people who appear and disappear, live and die in disorder.'

The State knelt on a man's neck,
citizens filmed his sadistic death
and the West's black working-class exploded in rebellion.
Half a mile from my house, the State tasered a man trying to escape
and left him paralysed.

Within a few months,
the government had declared itself against
Black Lives Matter, Critical Race Theory
and Michel Foucault.

Policemen from a serious organised crime unit in Hampshire
came before a tribunal,
covertly recorded making seriously fascist,
racist and sexist remarks.

In November, Johnson announced a four week lockdown,
heralding the Christmas lights at the end of the tunnel
that turn out to be the lights of an oncoming train.
Deaths spike way higher than April.

Schools cannot test adequately:
Call in the army!
Lorries stuck at Dover:
Call in the army!
Illegal New Year's Eve parties:
Call in the army!
The army offers a phone line if schools need support.
Polish doctors fly in to help.

Double the death toll in Spain and Germany
but this is not the time, says the Home Secretary,
to talk about mismanagement.
Lord Ashcroft's firm gets a £350 million contract,
directed through the VIP, no-competition, no-accountability lane.
National Audit Office audits that, in 6 months,
£10 billion was spent this way.

Borders closed but the horse has bolted.
Priti Patel says she will keep banging the drum
for regular deportation flights.

The vaccine on the horizon,
is the technocratic panacea for all the bumbling and bungling
and passing of bungs,
but new variants mutate beyond our control
and the epidemic which became a pandemic
now is endemic,
looks like it will be ever with us.
Life becomes more risky,
still socially distant,
in our isolated, closed-bordered selves.

Sam, educator, poet, activist

"I'm a support worker at a supported accommodation service for people with mental health needs. Supported living feels like a bit of a grey area when it comes to what precautions we need to be taking and I've been struggling with the confusion and uncertainty of that. We're not a care home, we don't do personal care, and all of the residents have their own self-contained flats that are considered individual households. As such, we have been told we don't need anything in the way of PPE. However, in practice, residents still come into contact with each other and staff frequently: staff observe the majority of them with their medication, they use the garden (not always sticking to the two person limit that has been advised), some are still going into each others' flats, and often, especially now that residents are understandably bored and the communal living area is closed, they hang out outside the staff office or in the hallways, keen to chat and engage. We've put in place social distancing measures, trying to ensure a 2m distance between residents and staff at all times, but in practice, this doesn't always happen. Most of the residents aren't following the government rules. They're still seeing friends, going between the scheme and their families' homes, inviting guests over. We can advise them on what measures they should be taking, try to reiterate the importance of following the rules, but we can't force them to comply (well, in theory, we could call the police, but I don't think most members of staff would feel comfortable doing that). Also, my position is that there needs to be an acknowledgment that for some groups abiding by the lockdown isn't possible, maybe because they have essential jobs that can't be done from home but maybe also because they have mental health issues that make following or understanding certain rules either difficult or (if strictly complied with) dangerously detrimental to their mental health. We have some PPE at the moment (gloves and half a pack of surgical masks), but as we don't perform personal care or shouldn't (in theory) have to come within 2m of residents, official guidance is that we don't need it. Initially, we were delivered a box of masks from Tower Hamlets (our borough) and staff were using those. However, as we weren't given that many, staff have been wearing the same ones for days and sometimes weeks at a time. We've also been giving them to care and cleaning staff who arrive at the service without it. Initially, we gave masks to residents too, for them to wear when staff went into their flats (which we do frequently to observe medication), and again, those that are still wearing them are wearing the same ones they were given weeks ago. Staff have bought in their own too. I have a cloth one I made myself which I wash and reuse everyday and another staff member brought in some she got online made out of a black stretchy material. I'm not entirely sure of the effectiveness of either, but am imagining it's better than nothing. I've voiced concerns to my service manager (initially when things first kicked off and then again recently) who was sympathetic and said she would relay some of my points to head office, but that we weren't a care home and weren't performing personal care, so therefore a lot of what I was saying regarding access to PPE and training in PPE use and infection control procedures wasn't necessarily valid. I talked to my union who suggested I talk to my colleagues and see if they'd be interested in organising an informal discussion.

Anonymous, Pandemic Notes Survey, 30/04/20 "

01

Intro

" I'm finding inspiration in my mom and aunt. They're both nurses, with my aunt on the front-line in NYC. Their attitudes don't come from an idealistic place, but a pragmatic one. "We'll get through this," my aunt said over a video chat, "because we have no other choice." It's an attitude that has no patience for selfishness or nihilism. I feel like such a dumb baby compared to them.

Anonymous, Pandemic Notes Survey, Q5, 15/04/20 "

When we heard the news about a new virus in China back in December 2019 we really thought it wouldn't affect us. We live in the developed world after all, we have access to vaccines, healthcare, and competent governments that will save us from this disaster. The vanity of our Western species at its best! However, the virus reached us, spread rapidly, the healthcare system was repeatedly overloaded and governments were not competent at all, like they never really had our best interests at heart.

In the case of UK, the country this workbook mainly looks at, the state response was far from adequate. Profit over lives was the clear message and everything left to personal responsibility. 'Stay Home, Protect the NHS, Save Lives' but 'Eat Out, to Help Out' have been the contradictory slogans of the Tory government. People were packing out the tubes everyday to still go to work, the track & trace system that they so expensively paid out for didn't work, the NHS was understaffed but they never wanted to invest public money in more testing, in health workers, in primary care, rehabilitation after Intensive Care, etc etc. Instead, the state narrative slowly shifted to lay the blame on the public. At the moment of writing this, the UK is facing the third inevitable wave of the pandemic! Deaths from Covid19 have now passed an entirely avoidable 100,000!

Simultaneously academia, scientists and journalists have been producing vast amounts of analyses and statistics to try to make sense of the total decomposition of our 'safe' and 'comfortable' lives. Analyses about why the pandemic started and the environmental conditions that will most probably bring more pandemics, analyses about economy, work, health, family, etc, statistics of reported cases, deaths, R Value, and so on. Wherever you looked tons of information about the pandemic was right in your face. But how were we experiencing it on the day to day level?

Pandemic Notes Survey

It was right at the start of the first lockdown in April 2020 when we decided to set up Pandemic Notes (pandemic-notes.maydayrooms.org), a website where people could leave their written or audio testimonies of their pandemic experience. We were so overwhelmed by all this, not necessarily comprehensible, information that it made us think that asking for people's testimonies and account of their lives under Covid19 could be both useful and practical on a collective level. We were witnessing the rapid change of our lifestyle, the deaths increasing day by day, the rise in domestic violence, the social reproduction crisis, especially with schools closed, the authoritative measures lots of countries were adopting to manage the pandemic and the grim future we could see in front of us. Being locked in our flats we felt the need to connect with more people, listen to their thoughts, their fears, the issues they were facing with jobs closing down, losing their loved ones, fearing for themselves etc. As we described the Pandemic Notes survey at the time of its hatching, we saw it as 'a way for people to voice their fears, hopes, thoughts, aspirations for the future, which as archival material can be later on used to understand and reflect on this past moment'. We also saw a use in being able to 'capture the moment in a critical way that lets us re-design the future by reminding us what our hopes were while in the midst of the crisis'.

When we started reading what people had to say, we realised that we had to do something with the wealth of personal stories we were collecting and something to help make those voices be heard in some small way. In the main what we heard was a rollercoaster of emotions. Panic, desperation, paralysing fear to feeling gutted, avoiding thinking about its presence to loneliness, will it ever end, how will it be after, are cats infectious, when do pandemics finish, will the vaccine work? And often back to fear, being tired of home activity, tired of Zoom, tired of being unaccountably tired all the time. A couple of months after the Pandemic Notes survey we also realised that these very personal responses to the pandemic were so important and hopeful. This is when we thought to produce this workbook, which, in some small way could be a contribution to bringing out some of the emotions that were born during this period, reflect the discussions we were having and record different community efforts to help each other as the government was failing us.

The workbook isn't attempting to present an exhaustive record of the pandemic in the UK. It's closer to a snapshot of different efforts and emotions throughout 2020 as we go into 2021. We are not 'experts' in anyone's life or struggles after all, just people who desire something more of this world and people who want to listen but also to share whatever we have learnt along the way. We also wanted to reply to some of the things we've heard with some critical thoughts and questions. In the making of this workbook, we also had to confront the social reproduction crisis in our own homes and one of us going through having Covid19. So the workbook is our timid effort to map the fields of life that were affected and the responses workers and the community gave, as well as think simultaneously about the future. We want to believe that this workbook will be a useful resource to talk about the pandemic in the future, with useful material to understand what happened, accompanied by questions to trigger discussions.

There are plenty of great similar efforts out there that someone can visit to get a grasp of this long dark period. The choice to create a workbook instead of just a record is because we would like the pandemic to be a stimulus for discussions around the state and our relationship with it, the power workers and communities have to respond to such disasters collectively and to think about what future we want so that we take the necessary steps to go towards it. We want this record of how people organised now to be useful for future collective organising.

State, Labour and Community Responses to the Pandemic

The workbook is comprised of three sections:
- the response the state gave to manage the pandemic,
- the organising efforts of workers to keep their jobs and demand Personal Protective Equipment (PPE), and
- the various responses different communities gave to support each other.

Throughout the workbook there are quotes from the anonymous contributions we got on the Pandemic Notes survey. There are also great contributions from people organising at work or the community, in grassroots unions, renters unions, mutual aid groups and other community structures, that give us a good insight to these struggles.

We have re-purposed various photos of anti-lockdown demonstrators by replacing their reactionary slogans with quotes we like, support and want to spread. Fight the power!

We have also compiled a reading list of books and articles produced during this period to facilitate the study of the pandemic. Unfortunately, we are far from seeing an end to this disaster, it is February 2021 and the majority of the countries globally are still struggling to properly manage it. We want to believe that all these efforts from the ground will continue the amazing work they have been doing and that this pandemic will prove a trigger to rethink our capitalist, individualist lifestyle to create a future based on mutual aid, collective organising, respect to our differences and love.

Though uncertain and unfamiliar, there will be a world after Covid-19 and what the left does now will determine what this new world looks like. Over the coming months we can anticipate a wave of unsafe returns to work, mass redundancies, evictions and deportations, and an emboldened and frustrated right-wing

Quote from 'Organising Strategy after Lockdown'
by Kate Flood

Why have we called this a 'Workbook'?

As part of the production of this publication, we organised two online workshops in November 2020 with different people active in organising in unions, housing campaigns, community groups etc to enable us all to chat and discuss what things were pressing and what things might help us imagine a future together. At the end of each workshop, we asked participants to list 'pertinent questions' they had heard from the discussions. We also wanted them to talk about whether they heard any 'practical or useful tensions' in what had been said about organising. As you can read throughout the pamphlet, we were also interested in how the personal and the political had been dramatically collapsed into each other by Covid19. This is often reflected in the contributions throughout, where different ways have been used to express how that feels.

From this collective work and in the spirit of a radical political education tradition, we have called this publication a 'workbook'. We have used the workshop participants' questions and tensions as described above as a jumping off point in thinking through what the publication could be like. We see a workbook as something more than just a documentary and a commentary of the current moment. Rather than merely stating our opinions and desires, as if they were definitive answers to various political questions, we are happier to leave questions hanging and waiting to be picked up and worked with by whoever reads this workbook. With this in mind, at the end of each section you can find a set of questions that, in the main, refer to the ideas expressed in the preceding texts. We thought it would be great if the questions ranged from simple ones to more complex ones hopefully allowing the workbook to be useful for different audiences but also in a small way to offers some challenges. We hope the workbook can provide something of practical use for individual readers and hopefully group discussions.

We also encourage different ways of approaching how to answer the questions we pose. Are there ways a group can reflect on these questions without relying only on discussion and the (disembodied) voice? Are there any exercises, games, activities and so on that could be used for group work on these questions? Are there different meeting structures that would produce an actual encounter with the questions rather than just a discursive one? Are there different time frames that can be used rather than single meetings? Don't forget about the role of play and joy in working together.

Finally, the process of reflecting together on political questions towards forming a shared analysis to act from also requires that a process of synthesis (turning your reflection into an analysis) is undertaken. Although a question begs an answer, we would also encourage that a question also begs further questions. That is also a vital part of any process of synthesis.

Using archives to answer questions:

Many of the questions in the workbook ask about historical struggles and what we can learn from them. There are numerous public archives that host tons of radical histories and reflection on them. Mayday Rooms is one. The 56a Infoshop in Elephant & Castle is another. We recommend also the Bishopsgate Institute and Feminist Library. There are also regional archives such as Sparrow's Nest in Nottingham, for example. While access to these spaces is limited due to Covid19 regulations, there are also many online archives that cover similar material. Again Mayday Rooms hosts a ton of interesting material and there is the brilliant website Leftovers (leftove.rs). Past Tense Publications website has a lot on various UK struggles too.

Pandemic Notes Survey Questions

1. What does the current moment feel like?

2. Have your living conditions fundamentally changed? (think about your work, housing, access to resources, childcare, etc.)

3. What's your biggest fear about what might remain from how we have lived during the quarantine? (think about personal habits, social relationships, conditions of work and/or restrictions imposed by the government)

4. Is there anything you have enjoyed about the quarantine?

5. Who or what do you find inspiring right now?

6. Have any of your thoughts or ideas have surprised you during this crisis?

7. What would you have done differently if you had known this was coming and what do you hope to do differently when this is all over?

8. If we could change the world after this crisis, what would that world look like for you?

9. Age

10. Employment

11. Town/ Country

Acknowledgments

A huge thanks to the people that participated in the workshops we organised to hold discussions on the issues presented: Danny, Chris, Sam, Susan, Sandal and Hannah, to all the people that contributed to the survey, as well as to Tom from IWW General Branch, George from IWGB UoL Branch and Ethan from IWGB Couriers for their contributions on the work chapter.

The Pandemic Notes project has been realised by Chris from 56a Infoshop and Fani from MayDay Rooms, and it was supported by Rosa- Luxemburg- Stiftung with funds of the German Federal Foreign Office. This publication or parts of it can be used by others for free as long as they provide a proper reference to the original publication. The content of this publication is the sole responsibility of MayDay Rooms and does not necessarily reflect a position of RLS.

About MayDay Rooms

MayDay Rooms was established in 2013. It aims to safeguard histories and documents of radicalism and resistance by connecting them with contemporary struggle and protest and to develop new free forms of dissemination and collective self-education. The Mayday Rooms building contains an archive of historical material linked to radical history. Alongside our material archives, we create and maintain digital archives and databases of radical history, with the hope that these traces of the past might freely be taken up and put to use in present struggles.

Our work proceeds from the conviction that social transformation can only happen when marginalised and oppressed groups can get to know – and tell – their own histories 'from below'. This historical work is a collaborative process, drawing together activists and historians from different places and different times, in order to make common cause, sharing experiences and ideas.

Our archival holdings are focused on social movements, resistance campaigns, experimental culture, and the liberation of marginalised and oppressed groups 1960s to the present: they contain everything from recent feminist poetry to techno paraphernalia, from situationist magazines to histories of industrial change, from educational experiments to prison writing. These documents challenge the widespread assault on our collective memory and the tradition of the oppressed. We aim to counter narratives of political pessimism with living proof that many struggles continue.

As well as housing an archive, our building functions as an organising and educational space for activists, social movements, troublemakers, and radicals. We also run a full programme of events including film screenings, poetry readings, archiving workshops, historical talks, discussion and reading groups, and social nights.

02

State
Response

> "I feel exhausted, honestly. When the government changed the slogan to "stay alert" I was like, hasn't everyone been alert this whole time? I feel like I've been on the precipice of a mental breakdown for the last three months. The government has totally abandoned ordinary people to our fate, and that is far more terrifying to me than the virus itself.
>
> Anonymous, Pandemic Notes Survey, Q1, 21/05/20

Do you study the Covid19 statistics daily and watch the Independent SAGE briefing once a week? Or do you ignore the news or refuse to read any analysis? At this point in time neither one nor the other seems to be invalid. How do we even know what's going on and who to trust or what info is reliable, what procedures to follow, what guidelines to adhere to that seem to change week by week? At the level of reliable and practical information, the state is simply failing us with endless U-turns on quarantines, lockdowns, school openings and closures, different tier levels and so on. As we shall see, the state is also failing us, not by accident but by design, when it simply continues under the guise of 'crisis' to enable the further rolling out of privatisation and future austerity programmes.

How has the UK state has responded to the Covid19 pandemic? There has been a series of chaotic guidelines, half-arsed lockdowns, tiers that are ever increasing in number and just a general sense that the state is not really enacting well their role as the authority that looks after the country's public health. The state has also put, or has been forced to put, into place measures to try and keep the population maintaining itself – paid furloughs for workers, the cancellation of evictions for private renters, an additional 20 quid a week for Universal Credit claimants, some opening up of hotels for homeless people etc. Yet at the same time as this failure rolls on day by day, the Government is also continuing on with putting into place new policies, laws and decrees. Statutory instruments that have no need to be 'passed' in Parliament and justified 'by reason of urgency', have been used to put into place new controls, new powers of surveillance, extensions to the amount of time personal biometric data can be kept and so on. The rules were also vague and discretionary powers were given to the police, who seemed to make it up on the spot fining thousands of people who had legitimate reasons to be outside. Fines and also arrests disproportionately targeted black and brown people. In the Summer 2020, white middle class parties in London Fields or Clapham Common were left alone whilst similar gatherings of black people, for example, in Burgess Park, were extensively targeted and harassed by police. The contribution from Class Work Project in the Community Response section outlines how in the work of giving out money to those who were desperate, numerous requests for money were by those who had been fined.

The state response has also been to oversee the continuing handing over of huge contracts to the same global private companies such as G4S, Serco, Capita, ATOS even though these companies have failed to produce functioning, useful Track and Trace and other vital data gathering and knowledge about the spread, and thus the containment of the pandemic. In the age of surveillance capitalism, the state and big tech monopolies go hand in hand both in terms of sharing data, and reciprocal manipulation and management of the public. Even though these contact tracing apps have not functioned well, just think of all the personal and private data these companies have now stored up for use and re-sale. It's vital to point out here that these big centralised privatised 'solutions' contradict what independent epidemiologist experts say – that small, local Track and Trace run by a well-financed NHS would be much more effective in reducing infection rates.

The state, as currently overseen by the ruling Tory government, continues to follow a distinct libertarian and neoliberal path. The Tories promise to 'shrink the state' and to allow free market ways and means to determine quite literally who survives the best and who falls by the way side. It transfers public wealth to a whole series of shady and disreputable global private companies reliant always on hefty state contracts, as well as a range of new off-the–shelf companies run by friends of the Tory party cashing in on non-tendered overnight contracts. A New York Times investigative article in December 2020 reported that '1,200 central government contracts that have been made public, together worth nearly $22 billion'. Of that, about $11 billion went to companies either run by friends and associates of politicians in the Conservative Party, or with no prior experience or a history of controversy… Around $6 billion went to companies that had no prior experience in supplying medical personal protective equipment. Fashion designers, pest controllers and jewellers won lucrative contracts. Public money that should have been put into staffing NHS, primary care, training volunteers to equip ventilator units, providing rehabilitation units for patients after ventilators, mass community testing etc. A friend working in a Covid19 hospital told us how old people were left unattended because there was no staff, dehydrated and hungry as there was no one there to feed them, having breathing crises with no support and losing them because no one was there to give them the oxygen they needed. Many old people apparently died because of loneliness and losing their will to live. Yet these details were lost as stood on our balconies or in our gardens and 'Clapped for the NHS' at the same time as the government was literally handing out bags of cash to their mates. This is what 'a socialism for the rich' looks like.

There is little new in the privileging of these companies, the private role in the state's expansion of the control, surveillance and disciplining of the population, the ongoing hostile environment for refugees and migrants, increasing mass poverty (14.4 million people living in poverty before the Covid19 crisis including 4.5 million children; 8.5 million working-age adults; and 1.3 million pension-age adults etc). Despite the seriousness of the global pandemic, the state has also not taken a break from their ongoing stoking of what is termed the 'culture war'. The state and the right-wing media have not stopped stoking racist divisions in response to the Black Lives Matter protests in 2020 or the arrival of migrants at the South Coast. The state and its media continue to fantasise new Brexit nationalisms of a 'Great' Britain (itself in part premised on the lie of 350,000 million quid for the NHS) and continue to demonise groups that speak out against the incoherent management of the Covid19 crisis. As we write, hundreds of thousands of teachers voted with their feet to keep schools closed, the state message was to attack teachers as somehow privileged workers with too much holiday and tiny work loads!

Whose Crisis?

In the age of what has been termed 'disaster capitalism', ever-repeating crises such as the financial crash of 2008 or the current Covid19 pandemic become the foundation for enabling further profit and accumulation in the increasingly financialised spheres of big tech, real estate, work platforms and so on. Even though the UK economy has been said to have shrunk by up to 1/3 due to the effects of Covid19 on the daily life of the country, it's certainly true that savvy capitalists never let a good crisis go to waste. Grace Blakeley writes in her book 'The Corona Crash' (2020) that 'the increasing interpenetration of big business and capitalist states promises to define a new era of state monopoly capitalism, in which the interests of leading politicians, financiers and corporate executives align'. If we add this to the future austerity programmes now being planned, we are not looking at too rosy future. She continues 'economic crises tend to be moments of market concentration, and the corona crash will see this kind of concentration on steroids. By the end of the crisis, there will be fewer firms left, and those that remain will be much more significant, in terms of both size and political power. The carcasses of small and medium-sized businesses offer juicy pickings for their larger rivals'.

Will the state respond to demands for higher wages, better public services and relief for the vulnerable by now claiming that these things are unaffordable, unworkable or unsustainable? We have already seen the rolling out of the absurd and infantile claim that the UK state, like a household in debt, has maxed out its credit card and so once again we must all tighten our already tight belt. On December 1st 2020, we could read three headlines in the same front page – that there would be no public sector pay rises, that there would be cuts in Universal Credit but that Phillip Green, the boss of the failing Arcadia Group despite asset stripping his companies' pension funds would not face any comeuppance. Want to know what the other side of the class war looks like: crisis profiteering, Tory ministers making short bets against currency and making millions, private jets leaving the country during Tier 4 lockdown, hundreds of empty prime real estate in London as the rich move to the second or third homes, it's Phillip Green! The communist journal Aufheben wrote in the aftermath of huge state bail outs during the financial crisis that began in 2008, that 'the appearance of a state intervening in, and against, the freedom of the economy was one with its underlying substance: the ruling class acting in its self-interest and to the detriment of the working class. In fact, the consequences of the government's decision to rescue major failing banks will result in massive attacks on the proletariat during the coming decade'. In 2021, the same analysis rings true.

What the Covid19 crisis has shown is how the new Tory administration under Boris Johnson has been both utterly corrupt with the handing over of billions of pounds to favoured businesses and businesses of friends, Tory party donors, relatives of MPs and so on. It has neither been hidden nor denied. Worse than this corruption, is that the next generation of Tories in power like Pritti Patel or Rishi Sunak (and it's likely that Johnson must be pushed out of office when the Covid19 crisis is over) will be the ones to follow their own libertarian logic and enact further savage cuts and privatisation of care and public health infrastructures, further rounds of pressure against wage increases, as well as ripping up oversight and regulation of favoured business sectors. It was no surprise last summer that the strong business lobbies such as horse-racing, catering and hospitality, tourism, airports and more had been able to circumvent public health concerns and get the green light from the Government to open up once more.

Simultaneous to this, we are encouraged to see ourselves as all in the same austerity boat and to cheer on a retired Army Captain who ran round his garden to fund the NHS. Wartime metaphors are brought into play as we are supposed to revel in a 'Great Britain'. Of course, all nationalisms love references to war and hidden enemies. Such reactionary narratives build further repressions as they herald the sanctity of the economy, waged labour, petty nationalisms, English exceptionalism and so on. We are also seeing the shifting of blame away from the state towards the general public who are now blamed for the rapid spread of the virus over the Xmas period. What can we make of this? Day by day the rules of lockdown changed, the rules of the Four Tiers were changing, the state encouraged us to keep on shopping, to Eat Out to Help Out, to keep the economy running, to return to work, for schools and universities to re-open. The state message to 'Stay at Home' was always a violent lie.

What to make of the ineptitude of the Government in handling the Pandemic? Writer and activist Gargi Bhattacharyya has recently provided a great analytically useful insight into how this shoddy governance works by describing it as less of a mess and more of a strategic way of undermining expectations to be provided with state-run services. She describes how the performed mode of 'Government incompetence is a contemporary technique of power that works to pacify the population, remove hope and erode belief in the effectivity of institutional response'. She continues by describing this as a strategy of 'inculcating despair as another technique of power that trains us to lower our expectations of the state by making the population feel bad at itself as a kind of technique of disciplining and exercising power'.

Our Response To The State

Yet there is nothing new or abnormal about any of this for those who have already suffered for years in this landscape: all of those people and communities already under siege from the continual restructuring of capital and the state's role in this; the weaponising of labour, the economy, race, migration, etc to aid the further rounds of profit and accumulation. Despite the Covid19 crisis, marginalised groups have continued to organise and resist, and it was brilliant to join with people taking to the streets to combat the racist nature of the UK state and its racist police. In those early days of the pandemic when it seemed so confusing to have lost a public space to demonstrate, the Black Lives Matter protests retook the streets bringing thousands together, toppling statues, resisting racists and fascists and fighting back against the overtly heavy handed policing of those demos. But even this could not hold that space as the pandemic worsened. What could people do despite a few street gatherings such as small-scale eviction resistance and groups picketing for unpaid workers wages? By Autumn 2020, the streets became the site of the dangerous mix of reactionaries contesting both the virus and the lockdown and calling for 'Freedom'. Although this mix of 'flag-shaggers', anti-vaxxers, anti-5G, patriots and genuinely confused people did not really take off, it does remain quite volatile. At the beginning of the year, 200 people gathered outside St Thomas Hospital in London screaming that Covid19 was a hoax. That's worrying!

We wanted to question though why the UK has not seen any decent Left or radical popular critique of both the state and what the state has done in response to Covid19. It's a difficult moment for critics of the state and/or government. We rely on the state for our public health and we need to feel that, in the absence of huge structural changes enacted at different scales by radical movements and communities, it will not just let us die or suffer. But, so far, the state response has been incoherent and chaotic. It has not privileged public health. It has decided to let thousands of people die. Yet wanting to trust that the state will act in your best interests is not the same as backing the state. There have been few calls for actual targeted suppression of the virus rather than blanket lockdowns that have not worked. We are caught up in the political deficiencies we have inherited from years of neoliberalism and post-politics where demands have become few and far between, and where the actual legitimacy of governments is diminished by their clownish figureheads like Johnson, Trump, Bolsonaro, and yet at the same time they remain popular. With rapidly increasing poverty and degradation of public support systems, it is inevitable that as the state begins to pull its furloughs, self-employed support schemes, Universal Credit top-up and ban on evictions, that we will need to come together once more with demands and street actions. It is also true that in other parts of the world, people have demonstrated both in the streets and with strikes against a lockdown that is premised on repression and further immiseration. These protests attacked lockdown not from a perspective of individualised 'freedom' but from the need to survive in states where little or no public welfare exists and where extreme authoritative measures have been taken. This public disobedience responded to the subordination governments have been imposing not to manage the pandemic but rather to establish their power.

It would have been great to have a really good radical response to the Covid19 crisis and yet it still feels like we are playing catch up to this idea. There wasn't really any popular public argument against lockdown that wasn't wacky and conspiratorial and premised on the notion that the state's response was a precursor to a fascist clampdown. Or there was an unquestionable idea that the lockdown, partial as it really was and, now is, especially in the Tier 1,2,3,4 iteration, had to be clung too because what else was there? Stuck between these two poles of reactionary thought and resignation, we feel that we have been unable to practically criticise the state's response to the virus. People did spring into action to make masks and hand gel for free to community members. People did begin mutual aid groups and solidarity funds, did initially maintain street politics with social distancing protocols for protests or they just took to the streets as it was impossible not to for BLM demonstrations. And we still trust the state to act in our own interests. But what would be beyond trusting the state and questioning the lockdowns? It would be something like not being against lockdown per se but being against the state, which uses this public health crisis to make our lives worse. It's somewhat amazing that the British Medical Journal can in February 2021 describe 100,100 deaths in the UK as 'state murder'. This is a public analysis already far beyond most Left or radical groups.

We were quite inspired by the text 'Thinking Beyond the Lockdown: On the Possibility of a Democratic Biopolitics' by Panagiotis Sotiris mostly because the paper tries to think of a way through the impasse of trusting the state. But also because the text situates the Covid19 crisis squarely in the reality that this and future pandemics are caused by the capitalist logic of accumulation versus nature. With nature viewed only as a resource and hence as a site of extraction there is the increasing likelihood of more and more zoonotic transfers of viruses from animals to humans. Sotiris continues that 'Despite the many different ways that the Covid19 pandemic was initially presented, we now have a sense of the multiple ways that it is linked to contemporary regimes of capitalist accumulation on a global scale. A pandemic is not merely or primarily a biological phenomenon; it is also a social process. Social relations of power and exploitation and regimes of capitalist accumulation play a determinant role in both the emergence of new pathogens and the social production of susceptibility and vulnerability. Infection is not simply about exposure to a pathogen, it is about exposure to a pathogen by populations that are susceptible in conditions and social relations that enable transmission and disease. Infection is not simply a biological event; in many respects it is a social process…'.

We need to go beyond the criticisms of the role of the state in public healthcare because the state itself is a messy and hybrid manager of capital too. There are a million takes on what the state is and we can't get into this here. But what we lack right now is the initial imaginary to make this a popular project for our own self and community care, and our own survival. Again, Sotiris writes about the need for a radical understanding of what is possible if we come together to continue, in some ways, where we left off when the pandemic hit in early 2020: 'Lockdowns have also been an exercise in imposing a form of undemocratic "state of exception" in the name of public health, whereas, by focusing on individual responsibility and practice, the very fact of implementing lockdowns tended to prevent any critical examination of the social conditions associated with the pandemic…in this moment, the notion of a collective "care for ourselves" acquires a new urgency. It points towards the need to struggle against the many ecologies of disease, exploitation and oppression engendered by the reproduction of capitalist exploitation, from climate change to the many versions of the contemporary "housing question". It points towards the collective struggle to move from the temporary suspension of some economic activity towards a permanent process of social transformation'. Such organising of our public lives against the state and against Capital begins at the micro-level, which is what was, and still is, exciting about the Mutual Aid groups, the Solidarity funds and so on. Yet we need so much more micro-organising at the level of individual streets, postcodes, in schools, FE colleges and universities, workplaces or communal public spaces. Sotiris writes about 'redesigning physical distancing and behavioral-change measures in ways that are more localised and adjusted to the realities of communities; insisting on behavioral-change based on consent instead of coercion, and avoiding the expansion of state surveillance; bringing forwards demands for more equality, less precariousness, better environmental conditions; demanding full access to health care, beginning with community-oriented primary care and fighting for public health oriented toward prevention rather than "security"; inventing alternative care and nursing practices to protect the most vulnerable; designing safe practices in all fields beginning with workplaces, in order to protect the people working there and to ensure that the necessary continuation of productive activity does not mean increased danger; expanding networks of solidarity; insisting that public protest and expression are essential aspects of collective "resilience" of a society and not added health risks'. This is what Sotiris means by a democratic bio-politics, where a politics of the collective body is put at the centre of any resistance to the failings of the state. With these few crucial points, we at least can see some sort of starting place and one which we can take much further. Public health is not just the remain of keeping us Covid-free. It is also the creation of alternative spaces and sanctuaries for those who need to leave 'home', while the government tells us to stay in. Or of spaces for people to come together to relearn collective repair, to breathe freely once more. A space where time is available via the provision of childcare, free food, learning and skill-sharing, listening to each other and so much more. The state's response to Covid19 has shown us that the future has to be of our own making. That is how it has always been.

> **"**Worried about surveillance of citizens - especially after the data collected by the South Korean tracking app was used to scapegoat gay men for spreading the virus. Also worried about police becoming more aggressive and being given additional powers that won't be taken away.
>
> Anonymous, Pandemic Notes Survey, Q3, 21/05/20 **"**

Quote from 'Desobediencia, por tu culpa voy a sobrevivir'
by Maria Galindo

THINKING ABOUT OUR RESPONSE TO THE STATE

When we say 'the state', what do we actually mean by that? Every day, we experience the state as both something that affects our lives (through its political will and ideologies eg. austerity programmes that want to 'discipline' the poor) and as something that we live (via its administrative role in our lives – as patients, council tenants, workers, parents etc). Whereas once, left-leaning parties attempted to ameliorate the worst excesses of capitalist social relations via the idea of a social democratic state (public investment, benefits and provision of services, council housing and National Health Service etc), we are now firmly in the age of a political consensus that both refuses to accept any alternative to capitalism. Forty or so years of neo-liberalism have been a concerted attack of the idea of the state as being actually democratic and able to maintain or improve the living conditions of the most marginalised. The recent destruction by those on the Right (including the right-wing of the Labour Party) of the social democratic Corbyn project has made this point quite firmly. There must be no alternative to capitalism and profit.

There are dozens of theories and ideas about what the state actually is and radicals have debated its role and history for decades but often with little input into actual class and community struggles. How do we make an organic and useful conversation again in our political lives? We have tried to come up with a few questions:

• It seems really important to us to ask this basic question:
What is our strategic aim with regards to the state?

 • **How do we deal with the contradiction of being dependent on the state for healthcare, for example, while simultaneously disagreeing with the way it manages the pandemic and puts profit over lives?**

• **How might we collectively even pose this question? Who needs to be in the room and where is the room in which we ask this question? Is it at school or college or university? In the workplace or in the local community centre? Is it in the nursery group or in the food bank? How do we make the conditions and spaces for this work of political education?**

Thinking about 'Political Education'

There has been a lot of thought and some action recently, both inside the Corbyn project, as well as outside in more autonomous groups and movements, on the subject of political education. It's not been easy as political education based on new ideas and structures and processes can only happen if we leap into the dark. Long histories of political education – community-based learning, trade union day schools, cultural experimentation and so on – have come and gone. We cannot base our future solely on repeating the past.

It sounds easy but, without a reset, it won't be. 'Political education' seems like we already know the answers and we can find them in big books or online lectures or from some of an older generation who have taken on the dubious role of 'political educators'. As much as there is solid wisdom there, there is also a stumbling block. That block is to continuously privilege experts with the role of political education rather than starting from what we actually know ourselves from our everyday lives and struggles, wins and defeats. We argue that political learning together based in the popular education method of 'everyone teaches, everyone learns', based in a wide range of formats, de-centering book learning and the lecture, would be one way of deepening and experimenting with how to do political education. This is also a much more joyful and inclusive way of hearing from everybody.

We are also talking about political education that works on our political imaginary and allows us to understand together where we want to go and how to reach there. We desire a political education that acts as an activity to grasp where we are standing, our position and our stakes, the injustices experienced, the privileges enjoyed etc. It's an educational process that overcomes the extremely academically acquired knowledge, the professional activists and thinkers. You don't need a PhD or a series of published articles to have an opinion about something. How do we question intellectual leadership, how do we restrict ourselves from exerting it? We need a process that empowers us to stand up for our ideas without getting overwhelmed by the 'wooden' technical vocabulary of the 'experts'. The pandemic has highlighted the problem of the authority of 'experts' who have bombarded us with ideas and comments that leave us disoriented and confused.

But we can also see that many people and groups are now talking about the inspiration to be found and the practical uses of 'popular education'. Popular education work has been happening for decades around the world but its most famous promulgator has the been the Brazilian educator Paulo Freire who worked in peasant communities for decades teaching literacy as basic skill in how to read the world and change it. His most famous book is the 'Pedagogy of the Oppressed'.

How might we re-design political education and what could we learn from the horizontal methods of popular education? We ask these questions on the premise that popular education is a process of collective problem–posing and then problem-solving.

• **What is 'popular education'? What are its origins? What are its basic tenets and processes?**

We find really useful the 'Naming The Moment' process of making a collective 'conjunctural analysis' to ground our activities and actions in a short, medium and long-term goal-based strategy. You can find more on this on 'Naming the Moment- Political Analysis for Action' by Deborah Barndt, available online.

• **When we talk about the importance of spaces to be heard in and spaces to listen in, why do we highlight listening as part of political and popular education? How do we learn to listen to people and give them the space to speak?**

• **How much do we expect people's understanding of the world to fit into our understanding of the world?**

• **What are the different ways in which people understand their own exploitation and oppressions?**

• **How do we create new shared vocabularies that feel rooted in people's everyday lives?**

• **How would it be for your group (or an intended group) to discover what these histories of popular education are and to dive into them? What processes might you use to share what you have discovered that aren't top down?**

Exercise:

Working with our political imaginary

One good starting to point is to get back to basics and ground ourselves in needs, desires and our imagination.

• **What would be an ideal society for you? Can you think of the aspects you don't like and how could you change them? What would you keep from the present day society and what would you get rid of?**

Work in a group and using A3 papers and colourful pens map out as much as you can the different parts that make up the state (ie health, education, social provision, transport, etc). When we look into these how can we see them functioning in a more autonomous, bottom up approach?

03

Work

" Key workers are incredibly inspiring, but they shouldn't be having to risk their safety to this extent, they should just have the necessary PPE to help them do their jobs. I was listening to a podcast about someone who worked in the NHS who said that her colleagues had started saying I love you to each other at the beginning and end of every shift because things are so uncertain right now and it broke me. It shouldn't have to be this way.

Anonymous, Pandemic Notes Survey, Q5, 25/04/20 "

In this chapter we're trying to give a snapshot of the responses and struggles workers gave to demand Personal Protective Equipment (PPE), resist employers' efforts for redundancies and other acts of exploitation at work during this period. This list of struggles is indicative and is far from extensive. Besides, the writers had to confront their own social reproduction struggle, which meant limited time to properly research and collect information. We also preferred the idea of giving voice to union organisers and workers so that they themselves talk about their experiences. In the contributions you'll find later on, members of some of the different grassroots unions present the struggles that were given in some sectors affected by the pandemic. With their campaigns grassroots unions have been changing completely the union organising landscape while the larger institutional unions failed to side with the workers. Sadly, what is definitely missing is the voices of healthcare workers, who due to their extreme workload during this second and third lockdown, when this workbook was being written, were unable to contribute. Docs not Cops and Nurses United have been doing amazing work around PPE supply and ethical support, amongst others.

As expected, work has been highly affected by the pandemic. Essential workers like health and social care staff, transport operators, education and childcare workers, utilities and communication workers, food and delivery staff were named 'key workers' and continued working despite the lockdown imposed. It is interesting to see which occupations were now considered as 'key', being applauded from our windows, some of them being low-skill, low-paid jobs that at any other time were neglected and even looked down upon. There are 10 million key workers across the UK, the vast majority of whom aren't able to work from home. Of course these were groups that were badly hit from the virus. 43 transport workers had died by June 2020 only in London, 139 deaths involving teaching and educational professionals aged 20 to 64 years registered between 9 March and 28 December 2020 in England and Wales but, while pressure is increasing to open up schools again, the Office for National Statistics claims that teachers were not at significantly higher risk of death from Covid19 than the general population. Restaurant staff, people working in factories and care workers had among the highest death rates, followed by taxi drivers and security guards. Nurses were more than twice as likely as their peers to die of coronavirus.

Workers that could work from home were encouraged to do so and on 20th March 2020 the government announced the Jobs Retention Scheme (CJRS), or else furloughing scheme, under which 80% of their salary would be covered by the state. In March the Self Employment Income Support Scheme was also introduced, which involved self-employed workers applying for a grant to cover 80% of their profits from the government. These moves were not made out of altruism, on the contrary it was a desperate attempt to curb rapidly growing mass unemployment but also a way for some companies to survive when they were forced to close.

All this might sound either controversial as it's probably the first time a Tory government makes such a huge state intervention, or suspicious, which is the real case. The Institute for Employment Studies estimated that 100,000 people could not be eligible for any type of government help as they started a new job too late to be included on the job retention scheme, while UKHospitality informed the Treasury Select Committee that between 350,000 and 500,000 workers in its sector were not eligible. And as Workers Inquiry Network says 'While the Self Employment Income Support Scheme may be able to help some of the self-employed, it relies upon profits reported in tax returns, something that many self-employed workers will either struggle to produce or will bear little relation to their income'. At the time of writing around 2 million people have so far applied for Universal Credit since the start of this crisis, when there are actually 30 million economically active people in the UK.

Women workers were hit 17 times harder than men, partly due to the types of jobs affected, as well as the issue of childcare with schools and two thirds of nurseries closed. More than 70% of working mothers who asked to be furloughed for childcare reasons since schools shut have been refused according to a TUC survey in January 2021. Bosses don't seem to understand or be bothered that the Covid19 crisis has been also a care crisis! Almost 50 years after the 'They say it is love, we say it is unwaged work' slogan of Wages for Housework is still so valid!

Big unions tried to collaborate with the government for the pandemic management and quite a few of them called off planned collective actions or ballots, for example the CWU at Royal Mail, the RMT at London Underground and UNISON in Tower Hamlets, showing their limitations and the side they have been always on. Smaller grassroots unions seemed to have been more active in tackling unfair dismissals and continue to fight to secure jobs and PPE.

Workers in the gig economy and/or on zero hour contracts, although in high demand, have seen their income dramatically reduced. As Benjamin Duke reports on 'The effects of the COVID-19 crisis on the gig economy and zero hour contracts', 2020, Interface Journal, 'The UK Government's response highlights how large corporations and the financial institutions were prioritised first, followed by established profitable businesses with three years accounts. Self-employed people working in the gig economy, alongside others managing zero hour contracts, finding themselves at the back of the queue. Such people have been largely abandoned by the state, being left to their own devices, having to fend for themselves. Employed people who qualified for "furlough" schemes found they had little bargaining power, having to take what they were given. Employment Tribunals were largely unable to sit'.

Angry Workers are reporting that 'In the transport sector, some workers took independent action against a premature lowering of social distancing rules in the London Underground, but this remained an unofficial and minoritarian effort. London bus drivers put pressure on management to enforce that the front entry door remained shut during lockdown. In early June, Royal Mail postal workers at Bridgewater depot went on wildcat strike against repressive management tactics against the union. Another more significant rank-and-file initiative was led by a group of construction workers and activists to "shut down the sites" – the high number of Corona casualties in the construction sector are sad evidence of the importance of that campaign...For some workers, like university staff, the crisis was used to force ongoing national industrial action to an end, with workers instead forced to work overtime to move classes online while their demands for better pay and conditions were kicked into the long grass with little to no response by the union...Casual teachers at Goldsmiths university took unofficial "work-to-rule" steps in response to managements' refusal to extend their contracts in order to make use of the furloughing scheme. Due to the significant share of foreign students, universities in the UK are hard hit by the global pandemic'.

In terms of home working, Workers Inquiry Network rightly say that 'For many office workers, working from home is actually involving an intensification of work. Many are being made to work harder and faster by bosses for fear that they would be slacking off at home. The threat of layoffs or furloughing means the pressure has not lessened. Facilitated by shiny new silicon valley tech, old forms of surveillance are being reanimated. One office worker we spoke to told us about monday. com, a remote working software used in their workplace. It allows managers to "centralize all communication within the context of workflows and projects." The app tracks, down to the second, the time spent working, as well tracking other key performance indicators. With the revelation that Zoom allows your company to track when you click away from a call, it has become clear that managers are using this crisis to implement more surveillance at work'.

For some this pandemic has been an arena of profit making. Amazon shares have taken off, pharmaceutical companies are playing games on our backs with their spineless negotiations, and governments' mates are enjoying public money without really having to work for it, i.e Track and Trace system. If it happened for you to have been on a job for long enough to access furlough you're from the lucky ones. Otherwise, many are in rent arrears, left without jobs or fearing for the ones they have, are dependent on food banks and school meals for their kids. For those confronting inconsiderate bosses, collective action has been the solution in various instances and this is what we will try and show with the contributions following from IWW, IWGB and UCU. Once again the power is with us and we need to wield it!

The thing about a crisis...

Submitted by a London-based English language teacher and organiser with the TEFL Workers' Union

I'm a TEFL teacher (Teaching English as a Foreign Language). I'm also an organiser with the TEFL Workers' Union, which is part of the Industrial Workers of the World (IWW). It's not an industry with a history of trade unions, strikes or - save a few notable exceptions - much in the way of worker militancy at all.

In an industry that epitomises a marketised, privatised, neo-liberal educational model, the pandemic and accompanying redundancy crisis has seen our union grow to hundreds of members. We are a small but effective counter-weight to employers who've never had to reckon with any sort of organised opposition from their workforce.

We just won, for example, roughly £100,000 in total unpaid holiday back from EF, a chain language school whose owner is worth 6 billion dollars. We've won various employment tribunals in regards to staff who were falsely classified as self-employed. We trained up dozens of people who acted as employee staff reps during their schools' redundancy consultations.

...is that it lays bare...

But we also shouldn't underestimate the challenges we face. Roughly half the TEFL workforce was made redundant this year. One big international chain, Kaplan, forced a 10% pay cut on their entire staff: even if you survived the redundancy cull, you had to sign away a full tenth of your pay packet.

TEFL schools love to talk about the company as 'a team', 'a family', but consider how the industry handled the furlough scheme:

The 'respectable' schools were willing to keep staff on for the first part of the furlough period. But as soon as the scheme began to require employers to contribute even a small amount of money to the cost of keeping staff furloughed, a tsunami of redundancies followed. It turns out that the only team that ever really mattered was that of the shareholders. The only family that mattered was the family of capital: investment, revenue, and profit.

Your manager's words about putting staff 'at the heart of what this company does' ring hollow when you know your school wouldn't contribute £20 a week so you could stay on furlough.

Having that understanding and having the confidence to fight back, however, are two different things. Most of our fights have been defensive. We win tribunals because the industry is such a joke that schools have just blatantly broken the law for years.

Pushing for things above which you're legally entitled means operating outside of a defined legal framework of grievances and employment tribunals. The next step: to turn the experience (and, hopefully, confidence) gained through these defensive struggles brought on by the pandemic into offensive struggles for things like paid preparation time, guaranteed hours contracts, and paid sick days.

...the reality of the employer-employee relationship.

The opening line to the IWW constitution reads 'The working class and the employing class have nothing in common'. It's this radicalism that's kept the IWW alive for the past century: people join because they want to keep alive the dream of a revolutionary working class 'building a new society in the shell of the old.'

But the influx of members who've joined through the TEFL campaign have largely done so because the IWW is the union in their workplace and their industry. This puts the IWW in the interesting position of - for the first time in a long time - having to consider what political education looks like.

In an age when the vast majority of workers haven't ever even seen a picket line, how do you instil the idea that, as a union member, you never cross a picket line? How do you draw the connections between the Covid19 crisis with the larger reality of a society in which every crisis is an opportunity for employers to tip the balance of power a bit more in their favour?

I'll end by saying that we've been supporting a group of teachers at an online school where the conditions are so bad we've nicknamed it 'the sweatshop of English language teaching'. The average age of the workforce is between 18-21 and these workers are some of the most dedicated and inspiring I've seen in my 20 years in the union movement. How they interact with each other, largely free of prejudices that were commonplace when I was a teenager, is heartening. Their seemingly intuitive understanding of the exploitation they face in the workplace - and the need to fight back against it - gives me hope.

I expect their generation will be shaped by the pandemic in ways we can't imagine; an experience they'll carry with them for their entire lives. If even half their generation has their same outlook, maybe there is some hope for this world.

IWGB Universities of London's lessons from the crisis - how Covid19 has demonstrated the power of a united workforce

Submitted by George, IWGB UoL Branch Rep

Organising and building power bears fruit – and recent developments at UCL are compelling evidence of this. Not only did the biggest strike of outsourced workers in the history of higher education force major concession from the University over the terms and conditions of these workers, but our power has also yielded remarkable concessions during the Covid19 crisis, demonstrating that an organised, unionised group of workers can achieve victories that would be unthinkable in comparable un-(or under)unionised workplaces.

Back in November, following an extraordinary strike by cleaners and security officers at UCL four main concessions were made, which have proved invaluable during the pandemic:

Cleaning, security and catering staff were given seven days additional annual leave from December 1st, plus additional leave to cover university closure days, to bring them in line with UCL direct employees.

It was announced that from 1 April 2020, pay scales would be levelled up for security, cleaning, portering and catering staff in line with directly employed staff.

From 1 July 2020, these staff would receive enhanced sickness benefits.

All other benefits would be levelled up in the next academic year - with all changes in place by August 2021 at the latest.

This constitutes the biggest improvement in outsourced worker rights at UCL in decades, and workers should be rightly proud of their efforts in achieving these victories. This work has continued during the Covid19 crisis, as the IWGB has continually pressured UCL and achieved a swathe of substantive improvements.

It is worth listing the demands we have won during this crisis following relentless work from the branch:

• Moving forward implementation of the Occupational Sick Pay Scheme that was scheduled for July.

• Special leave with full pay for all outsourced workers during self-isolation.

• Special leave with full pay for any Covid19 related absences.

The Covid19 crisis also revealed how precarious contracts leave the most vulnerable workers without any protection. During the first week of the March lockdown, dozens of Sodexo catering & hospitality workers and cleaners were told they would no longer have work and therefore would not be receiving any salary. This left more than 30 workers facing financial destitution in the midst of a pandemic. The IWGB launched a petition (with the invaluable help of UCU members) which in less than 4 days reached 1000 signatures and brought this to the attention of the press. Under this pressure UCL made two major fundamental concessions for casual workers:

• Reinstatement of all laid-off casual workers

• Full payment for all zero hour and casual workers, based on average earnings over a period of 12 weeks

This has only happened due to the heroic efforts of outsourced workers, the bold approach of the IWGB and the support of the UCL community, UCU, students and all the activists who have supported us along the way. These achievements are extraordinary, especially when some of these victories have been won during the most challenging times workers have faced in decades.

Whilst we knew that outsourced companies place profit before the welfare of workers, the translation of this into the disregard for their lives has been grotesque. During a major crisis, they abandoned workers and failed to provide essential support, often having to be pushed to furlough workers at no cost to the company. At many of the other sites we hold members, casework has brought some results to mistreated workers, but nothing compares to a well organised, confident and collectivised workforce.

The role that IWGB plays as a community focus point has been evident to see throughout this pandemic. Hundreds of volunteers signed up to support our members during the first lockdown, as a union we knew we had to shift to supporting members in extraordinary ways, skilling up our knowledge of the benefits system, alongside other things, to support our members facing the worst of the crisis.

This hasn't stopped us having victories at other campuses however. At the University of London all the cleaners came in-house after a relentless 10 year campaign, which also saw the in-sourcing of receptionists and security officers earlier in the year. This victory was a major vindication of the outsourced workers' bravery and their strategy of combining strikes with a national boycott of the university's events. In these challenging times for precarious workers, this victory brings much needed hope, and shows other outsourced and university workers a path to follow: determination, boldness, unity and solidarity.

At the University of Greenwich, we jumped into action when one of our members was suspended for challenging a student not wearing a mask on campus. The lack of clarity from the university around guidelines once again found a scapegoat in a low-paid worker. Our members at Greenwich stood up to defend their colleague, campaigned hard through social media and letter writing, and went all out to get him reinstated, which he now is. This mistreatment has been a springboard for the workers though, and they are now campaigning for in-house, and at the time of writing are balloting for strike action.

University management across London has never looked so nakedly engaged in a process of inaction and exploitation. Outsourcing has shown itself to be both a public health hazard and a pure expression of the contempt management has for the workers who have kept universities running. However, this creates conditions for a collective response, and our members' victory at UoL shows that with perseverance and the will to fight, no workplace is unorganisable, and no victory is impossible. Hasta la victoria, siempre!

"From March 31, I got increasingly more ill, but with a tight chest and difficulty breathing and fatigue. I was never deemed sick enough to come into the hospital, but I spent one month barely being able to walk from the kitchen to the living room without being exhausted. My lungs have still not been fully healed, I can't breathe a full deep breath, and the chest tightness remains, after nearly five weeks. My partner has also been ill. Our GP has been so kind and so patient, but my overarching feeling is rage right now. Rage at this government that did nothing to slow the spread of the virus, rage that I have been put in a position where I am meant to feel grateful for being sick and home because I'm not dying in hospital, rage that throughout this entire period I haven't been able to get a test, rage for every single person that is in the same boat and everyone in a worse one. This should not have happened. So, I'm afraid that my lungs will never be normal again. I'm afraid I'll never be able to run again the way I did before this. I'm afraid that when my pay check stops coming in June, I won't be able to get a job.

Anonymous, Pandemic Notes Survey, 29/04/20"

"Week six of the lockdown saw the complete disintegration of my mental health. I think only once in my adult life did I experience quite such a painful and prolonged period of depressive feelings. That was when my husband fucked off for a woman from work and rubbed salt in the wound with the offhand declaration that not only did he not love me, but after fifteen years and two children together, he wasn't sure he ever had. The first month of lockdown wasn't really that bad, most of the time. There was a sort of novelty value to the situation and then my children came down, successively, with chickenpox, which took up a good few weeks. Plus Easter and some rather glorious weather acted as pleasant distractions and made getting out of the house, or spending time in the garden, easy and fun. But then: week six. The temperature dropped, the rain started and any sense of novelty in being trapped in the house on my own with two primary-aged children requiring not just cleaning, feeding, tidying up after, entertaining, refereeing and getting to sleep, but also – heaven help me – educating. Having just had our five-year suspicion of the 8 year old's ADHD confirmed that week by a paediatrician (and experiencing similar behaviour in the 5 year old) the list of basic parenting is hard enough without adding in the pressure of trying to get the buggers to learn something. For nearly ten days I spent most of my time hiding, crying or straight forward shut down. For a social butterfly who gets most of her joy in life from being with other people, to be utterly without adult company for six weeks (unless you count the odd interaction with my ex husband when handing over the children, and believe me, I don't count seeing him as adult company) was soul searing.

Anonymous, Pandemic Notes Survey, 05/05/20"

'You must be busy during this lockdown eh?'

Submitted by Ethan, IWGB Couriers and York IWGB

Throughout the coronavirus pandemic and the resulting restrictions in place during 2020, this has been a familiar statement from our customers, restaurant staff and even friends. But the reality has been very different.

After Britain's first national lockdown was announced in March, delivery couriers like myself and my colleagues were lauded as key workers by the government and the public. Suddenly, we were no longer merely 'unskilled' workers, but recast as vital in keeping the country moving in a time of crisis. Our role in delivering hot food and groceries to a newly housebound public was now seen as vital in helping reduce social contact. We also provided a lifeline to those in self-isolation and the most at-risk 'shielding' groups. And some, including myself, delivered medicines to those unable to leave their homes. The Thursday 'clap for key workers' events were a surreal hallmark of our new status. More than once I found myself mid-delivery when it occurred, being applauded from windows and doorsteps for doing little more than delivering a pizza. It was charming, if not slightly discomforting.

But an apparent outpouring of respect from the general public sadly didn't pay the bills. The economic shock triggered by the first lockdown meant, in fact, that instead of receiving a boom in demand, our work quickly dried up. The demand for ultra-rapid grocery shopping didn't nearly make up for the decline in hot food orders. At the nadir of this period, I would struggle to make £30 in a day, even stretched across a number of different platforms – riders who only worked for a single platform, without access to others, were left downright destitute. Our days were characterised by long periods of waiting around in a cool wet spring, often for upwards of ten hours, eagerly snapping up our allotted one order per hour (if we were lucky). Those who worked part time simply stayed home. Full-time riders like me didn't have the luxury of choice.

This was all in the context of being outside, in public, where the threat of a then largely unknown virus loomed in the background. We were fearful of unwittingly bringing the virus home to our parents and grandparents. The de facto distancing I had to put between myself and my housemate ('can't be too careful') is a choice familiar to frontline workers during this time. Norms of social distancing were strict enough that riders also didn't socialise with one-another, weary of the fact that police were the only presence aside from ourselves in York's eerily empty streets. The nature of logistics work however meant that we couldn't distance entirely; the need for additional measures were obvious. But couriers like me are not employees but instead classed as self-employed contractors. The companies we work for – Deliveroo, Uber, Just Eat, and others – were under no legal obligation to provide us with the most basic personal protective equipment.

We didn't receive a single piece of PPE until over two months into the lockdown, and when these did arrive, they were nothing more than a half-dozen surgical facemasks and a few bottles of hand sanitizer. All the while, I made deliveries to places such as care homes and our hospital, places where coronavirus was known to be rife. Some outlets would disregard even basic distancing procedures, but we were in no place to call it out; one wrong word and our employers could gleefully terminate our contracts with no chance of appeal. We were left in a constant state of anxiety as our insecurity was brought into the sharpest focus, put at needless risk while carrying out our ostensibly 'essential' duties. To add to safety concerns, financial support was not forthcoming. Boris Johnson memorably said in one of his daily press conferences that the state would 'put its arms' around workers; for those in employment, the furlough scheme arguably protected many. For us self-employed however, the equivalent was a patchy 'taxable grant', not paid until three months into the crisis. Some riders were eligible. Many were not, including those who had worked the gig for less than a year. My co-workers who juggled employment with gig-work found themselves ineligible for support for either. Applying for benefits became impossible – I eventually gave up after being faced with online queues for Universal Credit of over 500,000 in length.

The attitude was clear – clapped in the streets, discarded by our government, neglected by the very companies we were keeping afloat. And so the mood began to shift.

As summer approached and social distancing measures slowly became laxer, riders began to use our free time to congregate. We would talk, share our respective fears and woes, trade stories and jokes, and start to form a real sense of a workplace community. While this may sound obvious to many, the importance of this in the gig economy cannot be overstated. Outfits such as Deliveroo and Uber rely on a fractured workforce. They instill an idea of enforced competition between workers; we don't work for them but are each a 'microbusiness'. When individual jobs are few and far between, their model is intrinsically meant to push a dog-eat-dog mantra, about as far away from ideas of community and solidarity as could be. But the pandemic changed this. The overarching narrative of a wartime-esque struggle meant that solidarity on the ground easily took hold. Instead of fighting over the scraps of work we were afforded, we formed a community stronger than anything that had preceded it, at a time where most of our meaningful social interactions took place at work. From this bonding outside our meeting point opposite a local chippy, a more formal solidarity started to take hold.

We had formed our local branch of the IWGB in January with an initial ten members. Throughout the pandemic so far, that number has quadrupled. Our particular precarity ensured that ideas of solidarity, community and shared struggle, in the context of a workplace union, began to energise an entirely new generation of workers, a generation well known to be chronically under-represented, in a sector that had simply never seen this type of activity before. Recruitment became somewhat effortless; the conditions spoke for themselves. Throughout the summer we got to work. Branches nationwide campaigned to highlight the neglect by these companies to provide PPE. Locally, we went toe-to-toe with our police force and won reversals of sudden £50 fines on couriers because of confusing and uncertain pedestrianisation rules – at a time where we could earn barely half that amount per day. We campaigned to ensure local restaurants provided us with toilet access as legally obliged, since public toilets were closed and frequent handwashing was paramount.

Our biggest action in the autumn led to a protracted boycott of a local chain restaurant over long waiting times and continual refusal to engage by management; in the gig economy, unpaid wait times add up to push our earnings sometimes far below minimum wage. We manned a picket line all ours of the day on Thursdays across seven weeks, eventually forcing Deliveroo to launch a review into the matter, with one of their biggest commercial partners no less.

We are very much just getting started. But this year, our union has shown, not told, the simple power of collective action. As contractors, we are not bound by draconian trade union laws. We can strike, boycott, or otherwise withhold labour at the drop of a hat. We can use not only our economic power, but also harness our newly enshrined 'key-worker' status to demand the respect we now rightfully see ourselves as entitled to — as all workers should.

Connecting up struggles in Goldsmiths College

Submitted by a Goldsmiths College UCU member

Since the pandemic started any remaining delusions about higher education as a public good or basic right have lifted completely. As students were herded back into halls of residence and many became ill and had to quarantine almost immediately, a kind of veil was lifted. It became obvious that the show had to go on so that full fees would get paid and so that rent would be deposited into the mostly off-shore accounts of the corporations who run student halls of residence -- rent for which many universities were liable if the rooms weren't full. The raw exploitation and violence of fully marketised higher education became crystal clear. A deregulated sector with no chance of recourse to public funds demands that cleaners commute on dangerous public transport to clean mostly empty buildings; it demands that teachers with underlying health conditions that don't meet the employers 'covid-age' threshold come in to teach students face to face, and that students who have nowhere else to go in the middle of the pandemic are forced into huge amounts of debt to sit in their bedrooms doing seminars on shitty corporate software that scrapes their data for future mining. Despite the exploitation, universities still haemorrhaged cash. Goldsmiths have paid KPMG (infamous multinational auditing and accounting company) a fortune for 'independent business reviews' required in part by banks to access loans, and in part to try get staff to accept that this time there really is no alternative. Management lay off more casualised staff, and are told they can be bailed out with government loans in 2021 only if they prove their commitment to 'free speech'.

In the midst of the chaos, the seemingly dullest of zones -- 'health and safety' has become something of a refuge for basic care, and a transversal line through which to connect the university to the communities in which they are situated. Trade unions are re-tooling around one of their original and most basic functions, and have found in the statutory mandate of health & safety committees some leverage to cut through the destructive ambiguity of management policies intended to ensure all risk is outsourced to workers. At Goldsmiths, 'Justice for Workers' campaign, GARA (Goldsmiths Anti-Racist Action), UCU (University and College Union) and the Students Union have held meetings with community groups and local residents in New Cross to figure out how to mitigate the reckless government and university policies of full return to campuses.

Despite the gruelling war of attrition that has characterised 2020, it is clear that deeper and even more sustained local struggle against university management and government policies will be needed in 2021. Already at Goldsmiths, there has been a vote of no confidence in management, students have announced a Rent Strike and UCU have just won a ballot for industrial action over the KPMG restructuring regime that promises to cut more jobs and make more misery. A curious feature of the last 6 months has been a preponderance of timely training sessions for university union organisers with various radical labour organisers in the US. UCU took part in a huge international 'Strike School' with Jane McAlevey organised by the Rosa Luxemburg Foundation, and there were smaller sessions with Labour Notes activists showing how the Caucus movements within trade unions can radicalise our work. Most recently, we had a really exciting session with organisers from BCG (Bargaining for the Common Good) and ACRE (Action Center on Race and Economy) in the US. Inspired by their work, 2021 might involve reorienting our union work now to develop concrete common bargaining goals with our local New Cross community, the rent strike and anti-gentrification struggles, and exposing the formations of racial capitalism that connect the gold in Goldsmiths to student debt and the cartels attempting to dictate the restructures to come. So much will depend on our capacity to share this work and take care of each other as the new phase of the pandemic and all of its horrors look set to kick in.

Quote from 'To our friends all over the world from the eye of Covid-19 storm' by Dinamo Press

THINKING ABOUT OUR RESPONSES TO WORK

Apart from the lockdowns and the closure of businesses that this has imposed, the government doesn't seem to really be taking care of the people. They are discussing cuts in benefits and services, more complicated (most often discouraging) procedures to secure Universal Credit, and rent increases, when the population has already been hit hard by the health crisis. Simultaneously we see a deregulation of working conditions, wage reductions, pay rises denied and an extension of Platform Economy, with the 'self employed' status gaining ground. What will be our response to this?

Reading the contributions from the grassroots union members we are wondering how many people know of these struggles when the mainstream media never play news like this. It's a great legacy though and a way to learn new (and old) tactics for workers to defend their rights. Finding out about those campaigns and following them, if not supporting them, is by itself a learning curve for collective organising. Learning from their successes and failures, their tactics and strategies can prove useful not only for organising at work but also in the community. There have been many examples of community campaigns being supported by worker unions and vice versa, something that increases the success of the campaign but also brings together the participants realising that their single issue demands, seen in a wider context, become more general and overlap. The following questions are therefore raised:

• **How do we map out all of those groups and unions doing work on this now?**

• **What are the similarities and what are the differences in how these groups and unions organise?**

• **What inspiration and lessons can we learn from the successes of grassroots unions (organisational structure, militancy, propaganda and tactics etc) that we can use in local community work? What lessons from local community organising (against social cleansing, cuts to services, providing alternative food and survival help) can be used for grassroots labour organising?**

• **Where could we find historical examples of this cross labour and community organising? What were its successes and what were its failures and why?**

Home working

Many people are slowly getting used to working from home and there is a discussion on how remote working might let firms save money on office costs. It's likely Covid19 will see certain parts of the work economy changed beyond recognition. Apart from the comfort homeworking might initially seem to offer, labour conditions are being changed forever in many ways.

• **Where will the current model of remote working (for many) leave us? How do we fight for our rights and demands in this contradictory world of enforced 'Live Work' from home? How do we talk about all the traditional unpaid work, ie care work, that has increased for those working remotely?**

• **What happens to workers organising power when they can't meet up together, suffer from increased online workplace surveillance while having increased workloads, a difficulty in separating work and leisure time, increased utility bills and other new costs that result from working from home?**

Online work has seen some innovation in tactics employed during work disputes such as the digital picket. Online platforms can also provide a different kind of space and time for organising meetings that physical meetings can't.

• **Have you seen any examples of where communications platforms such as Zoom and Teams can be re-thought as useful ways to work together?**

Unwaged and Benefit claimants

Traditional collective organising around benefit levels and provision have moved much more in the last 20 years into legal challenges via the High Court. Although these struggles are necessary and legal successes alleviate for many the gruelling disciplinary mechanisms of both accessing and maintaining benefits, such struggles remain abstract for most claimants and do not come from organising together as claimants and as a movement making its own demands upon the state as happened throughout the 70s, 80s and 90s and to some extent in the early 2000s.

• **How do the unwaged come together to make demands of the state, as well as support each other and seek support from those in work?**

• **What are the histories of Claimant's Unions organising at very local levels by and for those on benefits?**

• **What are the histories of Unemployed Workers' Centres that used to be feature of many towns and cities in the UK? Are there any remaining unemployed centres today?**

Contradictory as they were, often run by local Labour councils or big unions, and thus often acting as a brake on more militant unemployed and claimants desires, they were still maintaining a connection between the waged and the unwaged in struggle and provided resources, a space and a horizon to work towards further politicising claiming benefits as a part of the wider class struggle. There are histories of autonomous unemployed centres or groups, such as Edinburgh, Brighton and London, where more militant analysis, tactics and fighting back were enacted.

• **What were some of the main problems and tensions that were a part of organising with and in unemployed workers groups? Where can we find information about these tensions? What are the differences between claiming benefits in the 80s and now in 2021? How has the state's restructuring of benefit claiming over the last 20 years changed how claimants can organise?**

Exercise:

The social mask

Augusto Boal in his 'Theatre of the Oppressed' book describes an activity that was doing both with his professional actors and with the community members he was working with. He called it the Social Mask-Unmasking and is based on the idea that all of us are carrying a social mask based on our:

- Class: Bourgeois or worker? Bureaucrat? Manager? Landlord? In short do you rent your labour power or exploit capital (money or land or property)?

- Our basic social role (linked to the relations of production). Manager? Secretary? Policeman? Drug dealer? How much do you earn in comparison to others?

- Family relations. Father, mother, son, daughter, uncle or aunt? What's your relationship in the family structure in comparison with the position you occupy in the structure outside of the family, in the area of production? Is the father the one who earns the most in the family or is it the mother?

- Sex (as above, the structure of the sexual and family relations compared to the structure of the relations of production)

- The social complex family- neighbourhood- work. Neighbours, companions, members of the same ball team, of the same society for neighbourhood improvement, of the same class in school, of the same profession etc.

Try on your own to understand: What is your social mask? What are recurrent, typical social interactions you find yourself caught up in? How do you behave in interaction with other social masks? Does your behaviour change while interacting with different social masks or does it stay the same?

" With all these technologies of teleworking I am quite worried of the possibility to use this new infrastructure that have been put at the disposition of many companies to make of the working space completely unseparated from private life, giving the possibility to the companies of expecting a 24h availability of their workers. At the same time we must be careful of the action the state will take in regards with immigration and security as it is the perfect condition to increase the hostility towards migrating people and refugees, while our governments will take this occasion to endure the surveillance apparatus.

Anonymous, Pandemic Notes Survey, Q3, 24/05/20 "

04

Community Response

A few days of sudden jarring inactivity. End of the work-meeting-pub cycle. Almost feeling refreshed. Then a month of Zoom. Membership doubling. Adrenaline. The sense of a collision on the way. Re-emergence of a global horizon: rent strike in the US, rent strike in Spain. All the debates about 'organisers', 'organising', 'spontaneity', etc. filtering in from the US. Suddenly thinking about Rosa Luxemburg again, instead of whatever woebegotten Guardian journalist you want to 'brief'. Meetings encroaching into the daytime, then the morning. Terrible easiness of agreeing to more meetings. Can't pretend you're going to BE anywhere. 'Fine by me'. 'Good for me'. 'Works for me'. And the interaction with the state. Are we having an 'influence'? I used to laugh when Trotskyists would monitor government announcements for even the minutest change of course and then chalk that up to the tiny little demo that they'd held two months before, but amid the chaos of news briefings and fuck ups euphemised as 'U turns' it does feel like making some noise is having an effect. BLM in early June a shot in the arm of Covid-fatalism. Zoom-fatalism. This-is-how-it-is-now fatalism. First LRU in-person action in early July. The Sistah Space demo outside Hackney Town Hall. De-arresting a protestor and holding the road. Illegal evictions. The cops turn up and do nothing. Learning how to get the message across on the phone: avoid anger. Try to sound like a friendly lawyer. 'I'm here to help YOU [landlord] avoid going to prison'. The end of the eviction ban on 24 August. Snarls of new bureaucracy and government-induced stasis: 'the limits of reformism'. 'Zoom fatigue'. Really a deep existential weariness. Zoom rigor mortis. Wanting the meetings to end as soon as they begin. Hatred of the word 'capacity' (the inevitable image of your comrades as fucking Toby Jugs, filled up with 'organising'). A degree of mental retreat. Illegal evictions stopped in Walthamstow in October. Hackney in November. Things go on OK with or without you.

Danny, London Renters Union activist, Hackney

Quote from 'Social Service or Social Change? Who Benefits
from your Work' by Paul Kivel

> *It feels like a different reality every day in terms of What I Think Of This. But it does feel like abstract, useless things like career ambitions or personal status have melted away, or at least subsided. And the most important things, like friends and family but also things like food and shelter, become clear. It feels a little bit like an ego death, except everyone is going through it at once.*
>
> *Anonymous, Pandemic Notes Survey, Q6, 15/04/20*

Do you remember how you felt in the first days of the pandemic? Nervousness, fear, worry and uncertainty about what Corona Virus might mean. Did you have the feeling of not being able to concentrate? Did you feel like there was an ever-present background anxiety? It felt so individualised too. Would we get the virus? Images of the Intensive Care Unit became so widespread. Would we need hospitalisation and emergency treatment? Then a little later, as the virus was spreading and as lockdowns were introduced, came the threat of losing your job, the threat of eviction or of having to work in unsafe conditions. Some had it more difficult than others – newly-titled 'essential workers' in shops and services (previously classified as 'unskilled'), those doing working and childcare from home or health workers of all persuasions doing the work of saving people's lives.

There's an old cartoon that shows a man drowning in a pond. He shouts out for 'Help'. 'Help', he cries out again. No-one helps him. He shouts out 'Ten Pounds if somebody helps me' and immediately an arm enters the frame to help him out. The cartoon is entitled 'How Capitalism Works'. Despite how this overloaded satire on the profit motive rings true, there is still happily another truth of this world that if someone does fall over in the street, we will stop to pick them up and see if they are okay. The impulse is directly to care, and to care as part of a collective world of looking after each other. We don't demand payment for caring 'services'. We just intervene. In the following short text, we look at some care efforts that groups in different parts of London have put into practice as a community response to the Pandemic. We look at how people overcame that individualized anxiety and stress to start up numerous care works and infrastructures. As an opposition to the offer of 'Ten Pounds to Help', these practical and often radical interventions are also not premised on charity or the notion that care must be professionalized or in the hands of paid intermediaries to function. In many ways, mutual aid and solidarity denies the need for hierarchical-based caring institutions planting themselves, in grassroots fashion, in the very deep, nourishing and existing local soils.

Politics And Care

The terrain of the pandemic in the UK is the same landscape we knew well even before we ever heard of 'Corona' or 'Covid' - inequality, poverty, dispossession, health crisis, stress and alienation and survival and how those are entirely gendered and racialised. The organising principle of that terrain is profit first. Privatisation rolls on in the UK with a race to the economic bottom for workers as exemplified by multiple great British examples: The obscene scandal of private care homes, the pub chain Wetherspoons abandoning its 43,000 workers by stopping wages, universities staying open and insisting students pay their fees and rents, the platform economies deepening labour exploitation. At the same time, the ideological component of this terrain hardens to capture us and further divide us from each other. Academy schools (privatised education) make pupils wear casual business attire and have hundreds of detentions a week for basic infractions of these rules. What all these things produce are the conditions to be less able to care for others outside yourself and/or your family. Stress, anxiety, the lack of a horizon, isolation, stigma and shame focus your world down into the tiniest details of how will you able to keep going. It's exactly in this terrain that many of the initiatives we describe below have been created.

In the last years, it's been said, that 'Talk of care is suddenly everywhere'. It is not that there is anything drastically new being discovered about ideas of caring by those who oppose the violence of capitalism and profiteering. Radical challenges to this unequal society have always been rooted, in part, in struggle and solidarities as acts of caring about others. But instead and with the influences of feminist, queer, indigenous ideas (amongst others), care has come to be thought about as a primary grounding in how we might begin to build infrastructures of looking after each other at the micro-level and thus scaling up to challenge capitalism at its macro and structural level. A quote from the political arts group Ultra-red can help us join the dots between the urgent tasks of grassroots harm-reduction activism and the everyday violence of life as lived in the social relations of capitalism: 'In the area of public health, we draw on the history of struggle in AIDS-impacted communities. In a matter of life or death, people collectivize to build their own health services in order to make up for the failures and harm perpetuated by the state. Often that harm is an effect of state ideologies of racism, anti-migrant bias, gender violence, violence against queers, and the dominant culture of violence at the root of poverty and working class exploitation. In each of these instances, subjective consciousness means consciousness of antagonism'.

As the world burns, these narratives and ideas force us to think beyond the day-to-day economic survival and help us have an international dimension rooted in a love for each other. A quote from Feminist Finance syllabus helps us focus these ideas: 'Care becomes the social principle…as a set of practices built on top of the long standing ideas of cooperative not competitive politics in the everyday. Like how dignity is less about economic well being but collective power and horizons. How we are interconnected, how we are in common'. But as Feminist Finance also write: 'The COVID-19 crisis has both emphasized the critical importance of care and exposed its vulnerability. Not everyone has been affected equally and not everyone has the same opportunity to be cared for. The capacity of care is unequal and largely dependent on class, gender, and racial exclusions'.

If we look at the phenomenal rise of food banks in the UK we can see how such care infrastructures have spread far and deep into the lives of those at the sharp end of survival. We are never surprised to see that working class communities are the ones who innovate and extend free or low cost care in their own communities. Again, the caring for others relies upon those most vulnerable but this does not stop care from functioning. We recognise here the long histories of social solidarity, community self defence and self sufficiency, commonly organised by the most marginalised. These are collective nurturing and loving practices formed over the years in different ways and in different, sometimes overlapping, communities. In Southwark in South East London, various council estate Tenants and Residents Associations (TRAs) now run food banks from the TRA halls and as Covid19 hit they organised hot meals to be delivered to the most vulnerable in their estates and often beyond. The hot food often comes from local businesses or restaurants. Of course, we must acknowledge how the state takes this for granted and as it increasingly withdraws funding from social care, people are forced to step into care roles. Here again those with the least do the most to protect their communities and do it in a way where each site develops their own safety protocols for maintaining this work against the backdrop of the pandemic.

What has been beautiful to see from these examples of local food banks is the going beyond the provision of charity for people. These food banks operate, in some ways, consciously and unconsciously, from the concept of dignity. This way of seeing a collective community effort stems from understanding the power in coming together to provide for all, and to gently work with food bank users to break down stigma and shame, while placing users into a communal solution. Although the work is directly rooted in provision, there is a poignant politicisation at work here. It is in that politics that we could, as an example, begin to think about what would it mean if such food banks, located in fairly autonomous community centres, began to be seen as more active sites of political struggle. By this we mean that the use of these centres begins to encourage communities to discuss their own conditions and their own survival, and to come up with their own solutions. For sure, it is early days but these questions are being asked. Inspired by the Cooperation Jackson movement in Mississippi, radicals in several London boroughs are establishing and using food co-op models to bring people together. It's really about joining the dots between the basics – food and community, health and a horizon to be living more fully, giving people a breathing space and the incredibly important possibility of having more time to use as they see fit, creating community run spaces for discussion, and dreaming. Such autonomous spaces provide the most basic need for people that is to be listened, one of the most basic acts of politicised care. This is the very emotional life at the heart of political care. Such spaces not only produce a collective experience and pedagogy of how the state is lived but also 'Such spaces exude the sound, the image, the taste, and feel of the autonomy of social citizenship' (Ultra-red, 'State Listening').

Mutual Aid is back!

The incredible arrival of the UK Mutual Aid groups in the earliest days of the pandemic took many by surprise even though they drew upon the knowledge and practice of loads of people who have been active for a while. It's probably impossible to know why Mutual Aid, a concept at the centre of anarchist practice, went countrywide with more than 4,250 mutual aid groups being formed in the UK by May 2020. Literally a simple practical way of organising in your local area went viral. Although premised upon a simple structure of Whatsapp groups and a core set of practices to help those who were self-isolating or those who were unable to care for themselves, each group was able to invent itself as it liked. For sure, there were reports of problems and these reflected entirely the fault lines of a contemporary post-politics society where the day to day of people organising themselves has been shifted into service economies, charity or just plain doesn't happen. We heard of various Mutual Aid groups who fell apart once anything political was posted in the group chats. Or there were numerous attempts by local politicians, NGOs and, worse, fake NGOs set up by businesses to take over the groups. Right now, at the time of writing this in January 2021, the strength and the fate of the Mutual Aid groups is hard to pin down. How many of those groups are still offering the most basic help to those self-isolating? How many have simply ceased to work or how many are involved in conversations with their group, or even across local groups, about the next possible steps?

Again though, like our food banks example above, what was created was a possibility to go beyond the conditions of survival and to be embedded in the affect of organising together and to realise a 'radical relationality'. Mutual Aid tries in some way to break with care patterns as being done by those who are the most at risk. Such ways of seeing ourselves as a part of others' lives helps us also to realise that the sites of care are not only those of people's own 'home' and people's own family. For many 'home' is not a safe space. It is not a non-infected space if you are an essential worker doing deliveries or in retail. It is not safe if you have a violent partner and there were plenty of Mutual Aid groups sharing practical advice about support and escape. Josie Sparrow had written in an article called 'Mutual Aid Incorporated: '…A pandemic reveals something about interconnection and interdependence. It makes plain the ways in which we co-create one another. My health is conditional on yours. We breathe the same air, and exhale into the same space, and this space between us is also what connects us. We need one another, and, more than that, as Sophie Lewis argues "we become-human through each other"—that is, we are continually engaged in the process(es) of making and re-making one another. In this moment, where radical practices like mutual aid are at the forefront of the popular imaginary, the ways in which we ordinarily co-create each other (through isolation, loneliness, suspicion, mistrust) are exposed, as well as the possibility, seed-like, of something better'.

That something better has been the recent preoccupation of a few Mutual Aid groups who decided to rethink what political care and solidarity could look like out of the relationships built inside their local Mutual Aid groups. The establishment of the Solidarity Funds has been one example of Mutual Aid groups desire to go further. The work of the Deptford Pie and Mash Mutual Aid group sourcing food to give away for free twice a week in Peckham and Deptford is another example. Again, these are early days and the questions being asked in these examples are exciting – what does 'Solidarity Not Charity' really mean? In what way is it useful for the Funds to see their practice as 'wealth distribution'? How do the Funds plan for the next one, two, five years? What would time spent making a shared analysis of the current political moment produce for the direction of Mutual Aid groups? Right now it's early days, and we hope that Mutual Aid groups will go beyond the basics searching for new ways to organise in their areas.

Infrastructure As Community

Outside of the UK, the last few years have seen exemplary infrastructure building within certain major struggles. From Egypt to Hong Kong, to Chile to the USA, and now in the current farmers movements in India, a repertoire of tactics and temporary institutions have been initiated, shared, built upon as these practices have traveled the world. Street protests that have become a day to day fight against, for example, neoliberalism in Chile, have seen free food tents, street medics and clinics for repair and healing, spaces of conviviality for music and dance, militant street fighting tactics innovated, space held against the odds and the often messy experimental democracy of public assemblies. Such autonomously-derived practices challenge both the state and the moribund hierarchical forms, such as big unions and socialist parties, as being the deliverers of our salvation. The struggles are also not entirely based in the large avenues of big regional cities. Before and after the arrival of the pandemic, mutual aid infrastructures are also rooted in neighbourhoods. Tarlabasi, a neighbourhood in Istanbul subject to extreme pressures from global real estate, has long seen members of the Tarlabası Solidarity Network working with old and new neighbours in the district to forge a communal spirit and practical work together. One of the most common practices is the distribution of food and communal meals in their public spaces. Sam, a member of the Solidarity Network says: 'We would occupy the street as our space and pass down food hand to hand, physically embodying the far-reaching, lasting, caring connections made on the street table, extending into long hours of chatter accompanied by endless cups of tea following the meals'.

Yet in the UK, such major fights and struggles have not played out in such dynamic ways. We are very far off from that level of contestation. We are in many ways still shell shocked from the last 40 years of neoliberal decimation of our social and political imagination. Our sense of taking communal ownership of shared space in our neighbourhoods suffers from over-regulation and a lack of tradition in this respect. But, we hope what we have outlined above about the importance of centering care in our struggles is the beginning of inspiring new ways to organise.

Questions of public space, the scale of our activities and what horizon we imagine present us both with having to look and be clear about how to organise but also how we need a shared vision and a timescale for development of our strategy and tactics. The contributions from Goldsmiths College UCU member (Work Chapter), Sandal from Goose Green Mutual Aid Group and Class Work Project point to the need to un-find ourselves in what we know and take a leap into what we don't as yet know – that is how do we do the work of a 'common good' where that radical relationality comes to the fore. Following on from these questions, we would then highlight how when we go beyond charity and service work, and autonomous practice begins to spread, we will be faced with two important questions. The first is how do we begin to produce in our own areas for if we scale up, we can no longer rely on hand-outs and redistribution simply from our own pockets or friendly businesses. The second question is how do we prepare for the state's response when it sees its monopoly of power being directly questioned and undermined?

Here's hoping after the initial and long-felt shock of the pandemic, we can begin to deepen together these questions and come up with strategies and plans to continue broadening infrastructures of care and solidarity. This remains, of course, an urgent task.

Knitting Fragments of Solidarity

Submitted by Sandal Van Randall, irregular IWW rep

The beginnings of the solidarity fund are tied to the massive spread of 'mutual aid groups' that seemed to blossom across the country at the very start of the first lockdown; how these groups all came to the conclusion that anarchist terminology was useful or relevant to their often-liberal outlook was unexpected, but it did drive myself and others to join and in some cases set up their groups, in the hope of building something with longevity and a political objective too. Recognising that each mutual aid group was often only focused on the day-to-day running of prescriptions and food to neighbours, it became clear that there was an air to do something different and a desire to help people in other, more long-lasting ways.

The logic went; why not give them money and a choice of what to do with it, rather than just buy groceries? That felt more like an empowering gesture and not so much a charitable one; and that became the guiding principle of the Goose Green Solidarity Fund, which came out of several more politicised members of Goose Green Mutual Aid setting up a small pot of money for the community, and being at the same time anxious to not set up a distinct power dynamic that couldn't be overcome in later efforts. What was interesting to myself is that many of the comrades who became involved in the solidarity fund in Goose Green, and in funds that came after in other areas of London and the country, were newcomers to 'activism' or praxis. Many had come out of the Labour disillusionment that seemed to have become common amongst young leftists. Others simply had read the theory and not found an entry beforehand; I think that the simplicity of the idea was what attracted a lot of people, and the sudden realisation that we could just do it, we didn't need approval or a huge platform, that the Labour Party similarly with its huge infrastructure and reserves of money simply did nothing. Imagine a Labour Party actually helping people out through this pandemic! It was months before anyone in my local CLP mentioned anything to do with a coordinated effort, though I'm sure many were working to help as individuals. It didn't make sense to a lot of us that the party as a whole could just do now't; it does reinforce the notion that electoralism has died a death.

We've been very aware at the same time that a lot of us could do this because of furlough, because of being able to survive without working as we had been prior to the pandemic. This conversation about the power dynamic of wealthier people giving money to people who really do rely on it has been important, and we've set up a committee of fund-users in Goose Green to democratise the fund, make sure it's not just us with our blind spots giving out money and not really thinking it through.

We agree with regeneration magazine's critique that what came out a lot of Mutual Aid groups essentially became a microcosm of the service economy. This does not negate the incredible realisation and euphoria felt by many of us (and by us I mean comrades working in a lot of the mutual aid groups over the pandemic) that people weren't individuated to the extent we'd believed, we weren't entirely crushed by neoliberal propaganda. I think the phrase that the Black Panther Party used is particularly relevant in this context; Survival Pending Revolution. I recognise that the fund is not particularly revolutionary in this context; we're essentially a service for survival, although one which at this point is doing excellent work in legitimising a structural critique of monetary inequality - it's in the parallel work that we're doing, the collaboration with other groups across the country, the committees set up to help democratise the fund, which have the germ of the revolution within them. There's a lot of work to be done and this work has to be done in conjunction with other radical groups, to continue building the structures necessary that both empower our local communities, maintain an international scope, and a revolutionary horizon. Nevertheless, the fact that now there's a federation of six London funds and several others across the country, that we're now building links with all of them, makes this a project with a lot of potential, and a lot to work with already!

Quote from 'Activist Responses to Coronavirus' in
New Socialist

Finance Redistribution Project during Covid19

Submitted by Class Work Project

Throughout the Covid19 crisis the Class Work Project has been running a redistribution fund, during which we have redistributed over £380,000. This fund was established in the first few days following the government's announcement of a national 'lockdown'. Within a week our members had received over one hundred messages via emails, social media and whatsapp from individuals who knew they were going to immediately struggle financially, and were hoping that our organisation would have ideas, suggestions and contacts which might help in the short, medium and long term. The majority of these emails and messages came from people who CWP members had organised with in neighbourhoods over the last decade, others came from those who had come across the work we have been doing over the last couple of years via our education and publishing practice. Before we had the opportunity to think through the best way to respond to these emails and messages we were receiving emails from others who had come into contact with our work, asking whether we would be able to accept significant amounts of cash and get it into the hands of those who might need it.

Over the next few months more requests came in, as did the donations. The requests came in for amounts ranging from £50 to £15,000, each request was taken at face value and we attempted to fulfill it. Whilst we weren't always able to cover 100% of each request, we never offered less than 75%, it was entirely dependent on what money we had at the time, and what other requests had come in during that week. Donations ranged similarly, with some people setting up direct debits of £10 a week or month, and others dropping £10k into the account. We didn't set up a gofundme or make any public plea for cash. Our monthly newsletter let folk know the process that was being carried out, and there's no doubt that some individuals got in contact with requests and donations due to that. When large requests came in and we were unable to fulfil them, we contacted a small number of folks who had regularly donated in the past, asking if they were able to support us in getting enough to cover a request, but fortunately we were forced to do this very rarely. Often we replied to a request letting the person know we'd be able to fulfill the donation, but never heard back from them, and on other occasions we received a reply letting us know that they had managed to source the money from elsewhere, and wouldn't want to receive money that could go to someone else in a difficult situation.

The requests from individuals we had prior relationships with from organising work came from a variety of demographics within the working class. There were those who had been supporting their families via informal economies both legal and illegal, and had found themselves out of work and with no other provision available to them. Others had lost their employment due to the 'lockdown' and their former employers were refusing to engage with the furloughing process. Some needed one off payments in order to meet bills, debt and other direct debit payments were made; the fear of missing payments and fines being accrued was clearly intense, regardless of the statements made by state and capital that during lockdown this would not be the case. Far too often, but unsurprisingly folks needed weekly food paying for and top ups on their electricity or gas cards. As the 'lockdown' rolled on, we began to receive requests for sums between £40 and £300 for Covid19 fines, the vast majority of these were from young men between 14-25 who lived in urban areas where some of our members had been involved in various community based projects.

As stated at the top, in the end over £380,000 was redistributed from those involved in social movements and the broad left to those in the poor and working class communities we are from. Over 200 households received some of this money, and around 40 donated both small and large amounts. As of August 1st we have decided to stop accepting donations, and by mid-August all the money that has been donated will have been redistributed. Whilst we're confident that of the project's political validity, we want to take some time to think through how we've carried it out, where we've gone wrong and how we might be able to work a similar practice in the future.

We have been discussing questions of redistribution within our collective and at our workshops since we began in 2018. Our members come from poor and working class backgrounds, and have, over the last couple of decades been working and organising in radical left contexts alongside individuals from very different economic experiences. This experience has highlighted to us the ways in which economic capital increases the capacity for entry, and participation in many of these radical left contexts and the social movements they are connected to. Working and organising alongside those who have 'savings' accounts and inheritance which dwarfs the entire cost of our families and friends' life 'earnings', has always been gross. Particularly as we have spent decades watching those closest to us die due to poverty, and those that profess to be working for social justice and revolution sit on sums of money that could have saved our loved ones lives.

To be clear the process of redistributing money within the left is not a replacement for seizing the means of production and an entire dismantling of the current economic and political system. For any participant in socialist, communist and anarchist struggle this must remain the long term goal. However social movements are populated by those with a broad range of economic experiences and access to resources, and pretending that these unequal power relations do not exist, or that we can do nothing about them is politically dishonest.

Poor and working class communities have long history of sharing what little they have with one another, in particular, multiply-marginalised communities, doing so in the full knowledge that those with greater access to economic resources, driven by a combination of fear of precarity and liberal individualism, will hoard what they have. In previous blog posts we've discussed some of the issues that are present when engaging with financial redistribution. The ways in which the both giving and receiving of money is affected by shame and self-worth, in no small part due to the ways in which capitalism frames self-reliance, hard work and personal responsibility. The redistribution fund that we've been running over the last 4 months was able to navigate some of these issues due to the fact that people came to us. The majority of those had pre-existing relationships with us, and therefore an understanding of where we were coming from. There was trust that we would maintain the anonymity of those both giving and receiving, and that those receiving would not be interrogated or expected to offer evidence of their circumstances. In short, we would not be making judgements regarding their worth and deservingness of support. It's important to note that we are by far the only group doing this work, during Covid19 crisis hardship funds were established by and for a variety of marginalised and politically oppressed groups. Similarly, we've been in contact with a number of new localised Mutual Aid groups who were developing ways in which financial redistribution could become part of their practice. Prior to Covid19, the UK Mutual Aid F-book group has been organised around facilitating the redistribution of financial and material resources to individuals as and when they need them. This group has worked tirelessly to create an online space where requests can be made with safety and without demands that the request and the individual making it justify themselves.

We have critiques of how we carried out the redistribution project. Ideally we'd have been accountable for our decisions to more than just ourselves, relying on networks of similarly minded people and communities. We'd have generated the resources and an internal structure prior to the event, as it was we were fortunate when it came to resources coming in. The variety of ways people made contact with us, meant that sometimes individuals who were in crisis went days without response as we didn't check each organisational and personal email, nor old phones and social media accounts on a daily basis. The amount of time and energy the project took means that there are serious questions for us to ask about the sustainability of the practice.

It's also possible that we rushed into making several large payments too early, payments which we may have been paid a month or two down the line were often paid within days of receiving the request. This meant that when smaller amounts were needed in emergency situations they had to wait whilst we sourced the finances. The centralisation of the process was problematic, this type of redistribution project should ideally occur on a local level. Whilst our process was localised, with nearly 75% of requests coming from Nottingham and Liverpool - where our members have lived, worked and built relationships- none of us live in those cities presently. Perhaps the internet offers anonymity and therefore the security to make the request, but the goal must be to shift the individual problem into a social one, and this we would argue can most effectively be done on a localised level.

Over the next few months we'll be making a concerted effort to think about developing a better strategy to carry out some form of financial redistribution, it may or may not be similar to the one we embarked on at the end of March, but it will be directed by many of the same values. That those of us involved in social justice and revolutionary movements must act with collective hearts in the here and now, not merely wait for the glorious day in the future when capitalism crumbles. That we must challenge the dominant ideology regarding individual worth and the financial resources to live safely, both individually and collectively. And that we must leave no one behind.

THINKING ABOUT THE COMMUNITY RESPONSES

As we have written, tentative and embryonic mutual aid and solidarity work has mushroomed in the UK since the pandemic arrived. For those who want to look, the social fault lines of contemporary capitalism have never been more visible. Immense energies to act, to care and to look after people are being expended. In the book 'Dispersing Power: Social Movements as Anti-State Forces', Raul Zibechi writes that in the times of crisis what was once below the surface comes to be seen. Although Zibechi is writing in the context of two momentous anti-neoliberal uprisings in Bolivia, we think his overall analysis of autonomous and grassroots ways of organising are relevant to our current Covid19 times. Like the spontaneous organising efforts enacted from very early on in the pandemic, we see that the Covid19 crisis is, as Zibechi writes, 'a moment of rupture in which subjects display their capacities, their power as a capacity to do, and deploy them…Collective energies reappear in an infinity of instances, especially in disaster situations or those in which an individual alone cannot solve the problem. Does this mean that they are "sleeping" energies that wake up when needed? Or, conversely, are they energies that are being used and recreated within the intimacy of the family or neighborhood, in the gaps of everyday life?'

We feel that what Zibechi calls sleeping energies are also the energies that can never sleep. Every crisis is only a new crisis overlaid on top of desperate conditions forced from previous crisis after crisis. With that in mind, all radical political organising begins deep from within those myriad crises. A new crisis only brings to the surface all those collective and communal acts and infrastructures of care that have existed for years. Zibechi recognises this: 'The characteristics of a horizontal mobilization enable it to reveal the hidden aspects of cooperation that, upon bursting forth, displays what is implicit'.

What already exist then, spaces and practices of cooperation, are then magnified when we are forced to act to challenge ill health and death. Zibechi leaves us with a few poignant and fascinating questions that we want to use and think about here. Zibechi is responding to actual insurrections but we want to use his question as a way to frame how Covid19 produces a community response which, as ever, comes and goes, mutates and fades or innovates new political understanding and action. We also use them as a way to consider how, if there becomes a Post- Covid19 time, what happens to the radical infrastructures, groups and ideas that have been active in response to the pandemic. Do they go back to sleep?

• **'What happens to these collective energies and the non-state powers they encourage, when insurrectional times give way to periods of tranquility?'**

• **'Can non-state powers be institutionalized? How, in which spaces, and during what time?...Or, to pose a different question, how can non-state relations be changed into the natural relations of the present society? It interests us to know how social relations within the state give way to non-state social relations; how that path is reversed; and, especially, how both dynamics coexist in the same space-time.'**

For us, we read these questions as being about the danger of reformism where radical actors and practices make alliances with the state either expediently to allow a greater and more scaled up work to be possible or ideologically as autonomous groups are unable to keep professionals or liberals from taking power within them. We pose two further questions:

• **We live and exist in both the everyday invisibility of capitalist social relations (eg when we get paid for work or when we buy something) and in the mesh of the state at all geographical and administrative levels (when we see the doctor or send our children to school). Is it possible to maintain a radical practice of autonomy? What constitutes that autonomy?**

• **At what point do we become a movement able to contest the power of the state and to establish actually autonomous communities that can function, can deal with internal decision-making and tensions and that can defend themselves from inevitable counter-attack?**

In relation to the above questions of organising, we take from Feminist Finance a number of vital questions they have posed:

• **'When discussing forms of organising, the question of scale comes up. Should grassroots alternatives scale up to have a bigger influence?'**

• **'Localisation also carries within it the threat of exclusionary tendencies and the perpetuation of an inward-looking focus. Does scaling up change the community served by a specific initiative or does it open it up? Does scaling up risk creating diversions from original intentions and ruining imaginative contexts?'**

Mobilising Care

We are always interested in how different communities have come together to analyse their lived conditions and resistance. Making such a collective analysis proceeds from an understanding of what type of organising work and relationship building across community groups and members needs to be done. One of the ways in which communities resist is to put into practice basic care work for all those in the community. We can think about how these histories of political work based on the idea of harm reduction (clean needle exchange programmes, community-run health spaces, occupied housing, free food, extended queer families, women's aid safe spaces etc) are intrinsically linked to movements who have an anti-poverty analysis and poverty is intersected by race, class, sex, age etc.

It's poignant when Bolivian anarcha-feminist and psychologist Maria Galindo writes that 'Let's start by saying that dengue was already waiting at the door for the coronavirus, which has been killing in the tropics without headlines in the newspapers...Dengue and Corona virus greeted each other, on one side were tuberculosis and cancer, which in this part of the world are death sentences'. In our searching for inspiration, insights and practical ways of working can we look beyond the traditional political perspective that shrinks the World to very particular and often very disembodied ways of thinking about who we are, how we work as a collective body and what actual relationship we are involved in? There are so many more political, social and cultural ways to fight.

• **Who can we learn from outside our claustrophobic island and how can we reciprocate our learning from them, to give back with genuine acknowledgement and real meaningful solidarity?**

• **What histories and current political care practices are useful to explore?**

• **Can you find and share recorded community responses on the pandemic around the world. Are there similarities or differences and if so why do you think that is?**

You could research and make short summaries of community-based anti-poverty and harm reduction work and share these summaries in your groups and movements. Spend time looking at how, why and when these initiatives were produced, as well as how successful they were.

• **What social change resulted from any of these histories and what failures too? What were the models and processes they used that meant they could succeed? If they failed or fell apart, why was this? What lessons did they learn? Or did they fail to learn any lessons?**

• **Can you think of how you would have responded to the pandemic if you had the means, time etc?**

Exercise:

Listening to each other

It might seem easy, like we do it everyday, to listen to others but how focused are we really on what is being said to us? How much can we really hear when we have millions of thoughts passing simultaneously through our minds? Or how much do we filter what we hear through our own beliefs, values, prejudices etc? What's the difference between hearing and listening?

Make pairs and sit opposite each other with one person facing the other way. The person facing away has 2 minutes to talk about something that bothers them. Once the time is up the other person says what they've heard.

" … I've always been captivated by abandoned sites, states of suspension, off season feelings as a way of imagining how things can be different, or just putting a few dents into naturalised values and realism. Now the whole world has sort of entered into these states. Is everyone dreaming of a communism to come? Of course not, for the most part it has renewed a fondness for the familiar things we are now without. But there is a range of experience and impressions people are forming--maybe some of it we can build on, activate.. Unfortunately people do not become politicised by crisis or extreme experiences—these often reinforce existing ideas. The Corona situation makes me realise how vital it is to have ideas and critiques circulating before something like this—otherwise certain possibilities can never take and it will be their crisis not ours.

Anonymous, Pandemic Notes Survey, Q1, 13/05/20 "

Quote from 'Staying at Home' by Andrea Bagnato

"I'm very concerned about the extension of surveillance by the state and corporations, and the extension of police powers. It's all being applied in a nonsensical and arbitrary way that is causing immense loss of life and also further encouraging the atomisation of society. A beautiful 'hypernormalisation' scenario which is also handily reducing the future costs of the welfare state (casualties in care homes and the abandonment of disabled people) and handing over more and more of the NHS to the private sector.

Anonymous, Pandemic Notes Survey, Q3, 25/05/20"

"An end to half-baked neoliberal policies directing the most important parts of life; a renewed demand to take back our time—slowness (on our terms), reduction in required working hours (and consumption hours).

Anonymous, Pandemic Notes Survey, Q8, 13/05/20"

"More acceptance for introverts and our behaviours. We live in a world where extroversion is impressed upon us whether we want it or not. Social isolation is regarded as a disease that needs fixing but it's not the case for everyone.

Anonymous, Pandemic Notes Survey, Q8, 25/04/20"

05

Chronology

January 2020

The first two cases of Corona virus are confirmed.

February 2020

Cases of Corona virus reach 9 in the UK.

March 2020

The first death from Corona virus in the UK is confirmed. Cheltenham Festival is allowed to go ahead with around 150,000 attending. The Bank of England cuts its baseline interest rate from 0.75% to 0.25%, back down to the lowest level in history. Public Health England stops performing contact tracing as widespread infections overwhelm capacity. Local English elections and London Mayoral elections suspended. NHS England announces all non-urgent operations in England will be postponed, to free up 30,000 beds. Cafes, pubs and restaurants ordered to close. Nightclubs, theatres, cinemas, gyms and leisure centres are told to close 'as soon as they reasonably can'. The Health Protection (Coronavirus, Restrictions) (England) Regulations 2020 (SI 327) come into legal effect at 2pm, enforcing the closure in England of businesses selling food and drink for consumption on the premises, as well as nightclubs and indoor leisure centres. First UK-wide partial lockdown with police given powers to enforce the measures, including the use of fines. The UK's largest LGBT Pride festival is cancelled. The Health Protection (Coronavirus, Restrictions) (England) Regulations 2020 (SI 350) (the 'Lockdown Regulations') come into effect. 500 workers walked out of work at ASOS because the workers wanted to maintain social distancing. Bin collectors and street cleaners working for Medway Council's contractor, Norse Group, balloted unanimously to strike over a lack of protective clothing and unsafe conditions regarding the virus.

April 2020

The number of people in London hospitals for Covid19 reaches its peak. Occupancy of critical care beds in England peaks at around 58% of capacity. Occupancy in the month of April for Scotland and Wales will only briefly exceed 40%, while Northern Ireland reported a peak of 51% early in the month. To protect bus drivers, after their demands, Transport for London puts buses' front doors out of use, requiring passengers to board through the middle doors. Passengers are no longer required to pay to facilitate this.

May 2020

Black Lives Matter protests are held across the United Kingdom following the killing of George Floyd, a 46-year-old African-American man, by police officers while under arrest in the United States on 25 May 2020. The first UK protest is on 28 May, with a solidarity demonstration outside the United States Embassy in London. Hundreds of regional protests took place during May and June at a time when gatherings of more than six people were banned. Baroness Dido Harding, former CEO of TalkTalk is appointed to lead the government's programme of testing and tracing. The 2020 Notting Hill Carnival, scheduled for the August Bank Holiday weekend, is cancelled. The UK government updates its corona virus message from 'stay at home, protect the NHS, save lives' to 'stay alert, control the virus, save lives'. A new alert scale system is announced, ranging from green (level one) to red (level five), similar to the UK's Terror Threat levels. Boris Johnson outlines a 'conditional plan' to reopen society. Those who cannot work from home, such as construction workers and those in manufacturing, are encouraged to return to work from the following day, but to avoid public transport if possible. Outlining future easing of restrictions, Johnson says 'step two' would include reopening some shops and the return of primary school pupils, beginning with reception year classes. UK government advises people in England to wear face coverings in enclosed spaces where social distancing is not possible, such as on public transport and in shops. Teaching unions express their concern at government plans to reopen schools on 1 June, describing them as 'reckless' and unsafe. Health Protection (Coronavirus, Restrictions) (England) (Amendment No. 2) Regulations 2020 (SI 500) come into effect, allowing the re-opening of garden centres, sports courts and recycling centres. House moves and viewings are also permitted. A report on deaths in care homes in England and Wales from the Office for National Statistics finds 9,039 deaths between 2 March and 1 May, and a further 3,444 deaths of residents in hospital. In this period, Covid19 was involved in 27% of all deaths of care home residents. Buses in London begin charging passenger fares once again. Boris Johnson confirms plans (outlined on 10 May) for the phased reopening of schools in England from 1 June and outlines plans to reopen car showrooms and outdoor markets from 1 June, and for all non-essential shops to reopen from 15 June.

June 2020

The Health Protection (Coronavirus, Restrictions) (England) (Amendment No. 3) Regulations 2020 (SI 558) come into effect, without prior parliamentary scrutiny. Car and caravan showrooms, outdoor sports amenities and outdoor non-food markets may reopen. Gatherings of people from more than one household are limited to six people outdoors and are prohibited entirely indoors. Primary schools reopen in England, headteachers report a varied attendance rate of between 40% and 70%. Public Health England releases its report into the disproportionately high number of people from ethnic minorities dying from Covid19. The report finds that age, sex, health, geographical circumstances and ethnicity are all risk factors. Transport Secretary announces that face coverings will be compulsory on public transport from 15 June. UK government's ban on tenant evictions in England and Wales is extended by two months to 23 August. The UK government drops plans for all primary school children to return to school before the end of the summer term. Medical couriers who have been transporting Covid19 samples for multi-million pound NHS contractor The Doctors Laboratory (TDL) take strike action in response to the company's decision to make redundancies during the pandemic, and its failure to address health and safety concerns. Parts of the Health Protection (Coronavirus, Restrictions) (England) (Amendment No. 4) Regulations 2020 (SI 588) come into effect. In England and Northern Ireland, households with one adult may now become linked with one other household of any size, allowing them to be treated as one for the purpose of permitted gatherings. Boris Johnson commissions a review into the 2-metre social distancing rule. The review will be completed before 4 July, when pubs and cafes are scheduled to reopen. On the eve of the reopening of non-essential retailers, Johnson urges people to 'shop, and shop with confidence'. Black Lives Matter protest was cancelled in London after right-wing activist movement the Democratic Football Lads Alliance had called for people to travel to London to protect monuments. Protestors turn out nonetheless and are attacked by right-wing groups. The BLM crowd then chases various groups of right wing groups around the West End and to Waterloo. Secondary school pupils in England from Year Ten and Year Twelve return to school. Government announced that the trials on the Isle of Wight initiated on 5 May had failed. UK government announces that the 2.2 million people in England who have been shielding since the beginning of lockdown will no longer need to do so from 1 August. From 6 July they will be able to meet up outside with up to five other people and form a 'support bubble' with another household. Government announces that social distancing rules for England will be relaxed from 4 July, with people required to stay a metre apart but advised to maintain two metres distance whenever possible. Pubs, restaurants, hotels and hairdressers can reopen on the same day, but social distancing must be maintained. UK government announces plans to relax rules for England and Wales allowing pubs and restaurants to utilise outdoor spaces such as terraces, pavements and car parks, while outdoor markets and fetes will no longer need planning permission. Merseyside Police issue a dispersal order after a second night of celebration after the Liverpool FC won the Premier League title. Following a spike in Covid19 cases in Leicester, Health Secretary announces the reintroduction of stricter lockdown measures for the city, including the closure of non-essential retailers from the following day, and the closure of schools from 2 July.

July 2020

Education Secretary announces the UK government's safety plans for getting schools in England fully operational in time for September. The plans include keeping classes and whole years separate in 'bubbles'. The UK government publishes a list of 59 countries for which quarantine will not apply when arriving back in England as from 10 July. They include Greece, France, Belgium and Spain, but Portugal and the United States are among those not on the list. The UK government rushes The Health Protection (Coronavirus, Restrictions) (Leicester) Regulations 2020 through parliament to give police the powers to enforce lockdown restrictions in Leicester as from 4 July. The Health Protection (Coronavirus, Restrictions) (No. 2) (England) Regulations 2020 come into force in England, replacing and relaxing the previous Lockdown Regulations (SI 350), and giving the Secretary of State powers to make declarations restricting access to public outdoor places. 73 workers at a farm in Herefordshire have tested positive for Covid19, requiring the rest of the farm's 200 or so workers to self-isolate. Education Secretary announces plans for an emergency loan scheme for universities in England in danger of bankruptcy because of the financial impact of the pandemic. Health Protection (Coronavirus, Restrictions) (England) (No. 3) Regulations 2020 come into force, giving local authorities in England new powers to close shops and outdoor public spaces, and to cancel events in order to control Covid19. Figures released show that Blackburn is overtaking Leicester as England's Covid19 hotspot, with 79.2 cases per 100,000 in the week up to 17 July. Cases have almost doubled from 63 to 118 in a week. The Health Protection (Coronavirus, Wearing of Face Coverings in a Relevant Place) (England) Regulations 2020 come into force, requiring members of the public to wear a face covering in most indoor shops, shopping centres, banks, post offices and public transport hubs. Those who fail to do so will face a fine of up to £100. The Office for National Statistics indicate that England had the highest number of excess deaths in Europe between the end of February and mid-June, and had the second highest peak in number of deaths behind Spain. Restrictions are placed on Greater Manchester and parts of East Lancashire and Yorkshire prohibiting separate households from meeting indoors following an 'increasing rate of transmission'. ONS household survey indicates Covid19 cases in England are rising again, with an increase from 2,800 to 4,200 daily cases in the week of 20–26 July.

August 2020

50 million face masks bought by the UK government for use by NHS England in April will not be used due to safety concerns, officials confirm. Lockdown measures are reintroduced in Preston effective from midnight and following a spike in Covid19 cases, where England's revamped contact-tracing app begins public trials. Workers at a sandwich factory in Northampton are self-isolating following an outbreak of Covid19 at the plant. Prime Minister Boris Johnson announces a further easing of

lockdown measures for England from 15 August. Potential fines for refusing to wear a mask and the organisers of illegal raves are also to be increased. ONS figures indicate cases of Covid19 appear to have stabilised in England following a small increase in July, and despite local clusters of cases. Stricter restrictions are announced for residents in Oldham, Pendle and Blackburn from midnight on 22 August, preventing them from socialising with anyone outside their household, but workplaces, childcare facilities and businesses, including restaurants and pubs, are to remain open. The ban on evictions due to expire on 23 August is extended until 20 September amid concerns that thousands of people could be made homeless. Police in Birmingham report that a total of 70 unlicensed social gatherings, including house and street parties, were disrupted overnight. Greater Manchester Police reveal they have broken up 126 illegal gatherings over the preceding weekend. Far-right Britain First activists branded 'disgusting' for raiding hotel housing migrants. Small socially-distanced demonstrations against the Government's contract with Serco for Test and Trace which is up for renewal take place.

September 2020

Plans to ease lockdown restrictions in Bolton and Trafford are scrapped following a rise in Covid19 cases in the areas. The Office for National Statistics household survey suggests Covid19 cases remained unchanged in England for the week up to 25 August, despite local spikes in cases. Following a rise in Covid19 cases, social gatherings of more than six people are made illegal from 14 September, with the exception of workplaces, schools, Covid19 secure weddings and funerals, and organised team sports. Schools open as normal but parents don't have the choice of not sending their kids to school regardless if the have someone considered vulnerable in their households as they can be fined. Scientists and health experts express their doubt about Boris Johnson's Operation Moonshot plans to test several million people daily for Covid19 with a quick turnaround, saying that the laboratory capacity is not there. Anti-lockdown protesters gather in Birmingham to demonstrate against the introduction of tighter restrictions in the area. Campaigners in central London, many wearing scrubs or other NHS uniforms, held banners which read 'stop clapping, start paying', 'priceless yet penniless' and '640 healthcare workers dead, blood on their hands' alongside images of Prime Minister Boris Johnson. Demonstrators began a march to Trafalgar Square after a two-minute silence in honour of 640 healthcare workers who have died during the pandemic. Following a rise in Covid19 cases in the north east, local lockdown measures are announced for Newcastle-upon-Tyne, Gateshead, Sunderland, Northumberland, South Tyneside, North Tyneside and County Durham, beginning from midnight. Households are banned from mixing, while pubs, bars and restaurants are only permitted to offer table service. Collection of customer / visitor contact details becomes a legal requirement with fixed penalties, applying to operators of many types of business and community centres. The Office for National Statistics says that new Covid19 cases may have reached 6,000 a day in England, with a clear rise in cases in those under the age of 35. Prime Minister tells the House of Commons the United Kingdom has reached 'a perilous turning point' as he announces new restrictions for England that could last for as long as six months. These include a requirement that all shop staff wear face coverings, and a limit on weddings to fifteen people. Initial fines for rule breaking are increased from £100 to £200. People are also told to work from home if they can. Kent Anti-Racism Network (KentARN) organized a protest on Kent beaches on Sunday September 22 against the Britain First patrols. Couples who live separately are now permitted to meet up for sex, but casual sex is still banned. The second version of the Serco NHS contact-tracing app is made available for download by the public in England and Wales. 1,700 students at Manchester

Metropolitan University are told to self-isolate for 14 days after 99 tested positive for Covid19. Refusing to self-isolate in England after being told to do so becomes illegal, with a fine of up to £10,000. The change in the law comes after a government-commissioned survey found that only 18% of people with symptoms went into self-isolation. Fines for employers who penalise employees for self-isolating will also be introduced. Lockdown measures are further tightened in the North East of England from 30 September to make mixing with other households in any indoor setting illegal and enforceable by fines; the decision comes after Covid19 cases in the area rise to 100 in 100,000.

October 2020

Tighter restrictions are announced for Liverpool, Warrington, Hartlepool and Middlesborough making it illegal for households to mix in any indoor setting, including pubs and restaurants. BBC news reports that Covid19 restrictions are to be simplified into a three-tier system following confusion over local rules. 770 students at the University of Northumbria have tested positive for Covid19, requiring them to self-isolate. Fallowfield, a suburb of Manchester and home to thousands of students, is now the coronavirus hotspot with the most cases of anywhere in the country. The number of university cities experiencing significant Covid19 infection rate increases, such as Leeds, Exeter, Oxford, Sheffield and Manchester. The number of daily Covid19 hospital admissions in England increases by 478, the largest daily increase since June. London now has an infection rate of more than 1,000 new Covid19 cases a day, with 16 boroughs reporting more than 60 new cases per 100,000 people. The increase is thought to be partly due to an upsurge in testing. UK university staff prepare for industrial action over Covid19. Unions vote for disputes or strike ballots as more face-to-face teaching suspended. Five people are arrested and a police officer is injured at an anti-lockdown protest in London. Figures reveal that the number of secondary schools disrupted by Covid19 is increasing, with 21% sending pupils home because of the virus. This figure is an increase from 18% in the previous week, and 8% in mid-September. Protesters march through London to demonstrate against the city's inclusion in tier 2 restrictions. School attendance figures show that at least half of secondary schools in England sent one or more pupils home because of Covid19 during the previous week. MPs vote 322–261 to reject a parliamentary motion to provide free school meals to children during holidays until Easter 2021. The coronavirus fatality rate in England increases for the first time since the apex of April 2020. Eighteen people are arrested at an anti-lockdown protest in central London. A BMA survey of 6,610 physicians reveals that 37% hold the view that the recently implemented tier system in England will be an ineffectual measure Nottingham is to move into tier 3 restrictions on 29 October. Prime Minister Boris Johnson will announce a second nationwide lockdown for England on 2 November, with the restrictions coming into force as early as 4 November and lasting until December.

November 2020

Student rent struggles and strikes begin or continue in universities at Bristol, Manchester, Glasgow, Cambridge. Over 1,400 students are taking part in a rent strike in Bristol that began in October. Cleaners & Allied Independent Workers Union (CAIWU) organised workers at Facebook win against a restructuring and redundancy programme by outsourced contractors Bidvest Noonan. A potential rebellion from some of the PM's backbench MPs starts being angry at lockdown measures, which they describe as 'disastrous' to the economy. Up to 80 Tory MPs may vote against the measures when they are debated in Parliament. Transport for London secures a £1.8bn government bailout to keep bus and tube services running until March 2021. Chancellor announces that self-employed people will be able to claim 80% of their earnings during the lockdown period. Universities advise students not to return home during the lockdown, even if their courses are switched to being taught online. Parents United has called for a parents' strike on Thursday against the Johnson government's refusal to close schools amid a coronavirus pandemic already claiming almost 400 lives a day. As England's second lockdown begins, the UK Statistics Authority criticises the government over the way it presented data estimating potential Covid19 deaths to justify the measures at the 31 October Downing Street press conference, and calls for greater transparency of data and the way projections are made. The University of Manchester apologises after large metal fences were erected around halls of residence on its Fallowfield campus without warning. The fences are removed again following protests from several hundred students. Police break up an anti-lockdown protest in central London as 104 are arrested. Treasury would allow the scheme to run for a full year by continuing to pay 80% of temporarily laid-off workers' wages until 31 March. Sunak also announced an expansion in funding for self-employed workers from November to January. Organisers of a Manchester anti-lockdown demonstration involving 600 people are issued with a £10,000 fine. Fourteen people are arrested at an anti-lockdown protest in Bristol and sixteen at a demonstration in Liverpool. BBC investigation has found that Serco NHS Test and Trace is reaching as little as half of those identified as close contacts in some areas. Downing Street confirms plans to introduce a tougher three-tier system of Covid19 restrictions for England when the lockdown ends on 2 December. Dozens of arrests are made after hundreds attend anti-lockdown protest in Liverpool, and other parts of England. Prime Minister confirms that Three Tiers lockdown system will return once the lockdown expires on 2 December, but with toughened measures for each area. The tier status of each region will be reviewed every 14 days, with the regional approach scheduled to last until March 2021. England's new tier system is announced, coming into force on 2 December. Most of the country, including London and Liverpool, is put into tier 2, while large parts of the Midlands, North East and North West, including Greater Manchester and Birmingham, are put into tier 3. Only the Isle of Wight, Cornwall and the Isles of Scilly are placed into tier 1. Data for 19–21 November shows that cases are falling in every part of England. More than 150 people are arrested at an anti-lockdown protest in London's West End.

December 2020

British Airways staff vote overwhelmingly to strike. Around 850 workers at British Airways (BA) cargo handling company have voted almost unanimously to take strike action over the airlines' plans to fire and rehire the entire workforce on inferior terms. A vote of 350 UK bus drivers at the First Bus Bowling Back Lane in Bradford produced an 85 percent majority in favour of a strike. The drivers are calling for the pre-pandemic work schedule to be restored. MPs vote 291–78 in favour of introducing England's tough new Covid19 tier system, with 55 backbench Conservatives voting against the government, while another 16 abstain. Independent Workers Union of Great Britain (IWGB) is to ballot security officers, porters and cleaners for strike action at the University of Greenwich. Figures from the Office for National Statistics indicate Covid19 rates are falling in every part of England apart from the North East, with 1 in 105 people having the virus in the week up to 28 November, down from 1 in 85 the week before. GP surgeries will receive supplies of the Pfizer/BioNTech vaccine on 14 December, and have been told to have vaccination centres staffed and ready to deliver the vaccine within three and a half days of that date. The first weekend following the end of lockdown sees an influx of shoppers to high streets as stores hold pre-Christmas sales. Health Secretary urges Londoners to adhere to Covid19 regulations as cases rise in London. National Education Union (NEU) calls off a planned six-day strike over December and January at Kingsway Primary School in Wirral, Merseyside. More than 85 percent of NEU members at Kingsway Primary had voted to strike. The action would have been the first official Covid19-related strike called by the National Education Union (NEU), as pressure from educators and parents mounts to close unsafe schools. Figures from the Office for National Statistics for the week ending 5 December indicate Covid19 cases in England are continuing to fall, apart from London and the East of England. Thousands of Christmas shoppers descend on central London following warnings from the Mayor of London, and the police reminds that people should respect Covid19 regulations. United Voices of the World (UVW) union have a big victory to report at Great Ormond Street Hospital, where hundreds of outsourced staff are now being brought in to direct NHS employment. Their other main campaign at the moment is at Sage nursing home in North London, where staff have voted to strike over pay, union recognition, sick pay and annual leave. After Greenwich Council writes to headteachers asking them to move classes online amid rising Covid19 cases, Education Secretary Gavin Williamson orders the authority to keep schools open or face legal action. It is reported that nearly 90% of hospital beds in England are full and that health trusts face the prospect of suspending non-Covid19 treatment. Government announces that London, South East and East of England are to go into new Tier 4 restrictions. Anti-lockdown protests are held in cities across the country, with police making 27 arrests at a protest in London. UK's chief scientific adviser, suggests that more areas of England will need to go into Tier 4 restrictions to combat the new variant of Covid19. Tier four restrictions are extended in England after rules are briefly relaxed for Christmas Day. 50,000+ daily new infections logged by end of December.

January 2021

Brian Pinker, 82, becomes the first person to receive the Oxford/AstraZeneca Covid19 vaccine as vaccinations begin in the UK. On the 14 January the UK announces a travel ban on arrivals from South America, Portugal and Cape Verde. Schools didn't open after Xmas.

February 2021

Health Secretary Matt Hancock announces that people required to quarantine in government authorised hotels from 15 February will be required to pay £1,750 for a ten day stay. 400 asylum seekers are housed in Napier Barracks, an old army camp near Folkestone. 100 cases of Covid19 are reported among the asylum seekers many of whom are forced to share rooms and amenities with those infected. Local migrant support groups bring food and make pressure to close the camp. On the 12 February figures from the Office for National Statistics show the UK economy shrank by 9.9% in 2020, the largest economic contraction on record.

06

Suggested Reading

State Response

• NetPol and Undercover Research Group have been running a 'Policing The Corona State' blog (https://policing-the-corona-state.blog/).

• We also recommend the work of Statewatch who have been researching and analysing what the state does from many angles – migration, policing, austerity etc. (https://www.statewatch.org/).

Work

• Lots of analysis of workers response to Covid19 in the UK and internationally at the Angry Workers website (https://www.angryworkers.org/).

• Goldsmiths Mutual Aid is one example of a university based hardship fund providing money to precarious staff at Goldsmiths, whose employment has been cut during Covid19 and who may be further impacted by strike deductions during the 2021 Goldsmiths UCU industrial action (https://opencollective.com/goldsmithsmutualaid).

• Docs Not Cops is a campaign group of NHS professionals and patients who believe health is a right and not a privilege (http://www.docsnotcops.co.uk/).

• Notes From Below website has a collection of workers inquiries into work and Covid19 and how it affects all types of workers (https://notesfrombelow.org/).

Community Response

• Komun Academy have a series of interviews with political organizers doing mutual aid and solidarity work against Covid19 in different countries (https://komun-academy.com/).

> Building Solidarity During This Crisis (and the Next), Dean Spade, Verso (2020)

> Mutual Aid, Incorporated by josie sparrow (https://newsocialist.org.uk/mutual-aid-incorporated/)

> Organising Strategy after Lockdown by Kate Flood (http://newsocialist.org.uk/organising-strategy-after-lockdown/).

> Thinking Beyond the Lockdown: On the Possibility of a Democratic Biopolitics by Panagiotis Sotiris. Paper at Historical Materialism, London 2020.

• MayDay Rooms have created a series of archival scrapbooks where you can find material on community-based anti-poverty and harm reduction work (maydayrooms.org/scrapbooks).

Care Politics

> Social Reproduction and the Pandemic with Tithi Bhattacharya (https://www.dissentmagazine.org/online_articles/social-reproduction-and-the-pandemic-with-tithi-bhattacharya).

> Feminism, the Pandemic, and What Comes Next by Lucía Cavallero and Verónica Gago (https://www.rosalux.de/en/news/id/42112/feminism-the-pandemic-and-what-comes-next?cHash=97e64aad127bbeaa15ab82baa8d23d31).

> The Care Manifesto, The Politics of Interdependence, The Care Collective, Verso (2020)

• QueerCare is a transfeminist autonomous care organisation, providing training, support and advocacy for trans and queer people in the UK (and further afield) (https://wiki.queercare.network/Main_Page).

• Lots of stuff on politics, organising, care and Covid19 at the Pirate Care syllabus website (https://syllabus.pirate.care/). Lots of good takes also at Feminist Finance Syllabus (https://networkcultures.org/wp-content/uploads/2020/10/201012-FFZINE-SYLLABUS.pdf).

Political Education

• Class Work Project is a workers' co-operative organising around class, producing the journal Lumpen, publishing work from poor and working-class writers. They also run workshops exploring different experiences of class and the ways in which it is reproduced in our communities and organisations. They are also running extensive solidarity funds (https://www.theclassworkproject.com/).

> Pedagogy of the Oppressed by Paulo Feire. One of the starting building blocks of popular education. Theoretical but practical.

> Theatre of the Oppressed by Augusto Boal. A practical set of dramatic techniques whose purpose is to bring to light systemic exploitation and oppression within common situations.

> Radical Education Workbook is a wide-ranging look at key concepts, histories and practices within radical education and also reflections about the relevance of these ideas and methods to our struggles today (http://undercommoning.org/wp-content/uploads/2015/06/ref-workbook.pdf).

Covid19 Analysis

• Chaung Journal was written the excellent text 'Social Contagion: Microbiological Class War in China' that analyses the pandemic from within the intense structural changes of the last 50 years. As the secular crisis of capitalism takes on a seemingly non-economic character, new epidemics, famines, floods and other "natural" disasters, we can expect more and more disasters (https://chuangcn.org/2020/02/social-contagion/).

> This is a Global Pandemic – Let's Treat it as Such by Adam Hanieh on the COVID-19 pandemic (https://www.versobooks.com/blogs/4623-this-is-a-global-pandemic-let-s-treat-it-as-such).

> Seven Theses On Social Reproduction and the Covid-19 Pandemic by the Marxist Feminist Collective (https://spectrejournal.com/seven-theses-on-social-reproduction-and-the-covid-19-pandemic/).

> Corona, Climate, Chronic Emergency, War Communism in the Twenty-First Century by Andreas Malm, Verso (2020)

Resources

Lots of stuff at the Virtual Social Centre website including community and mutual aid resources, tools and so on (https://virtualsocialcentre.org.uk/).

NOTES